A-LEVEL

US Government
& Politics

Paul Fairclough

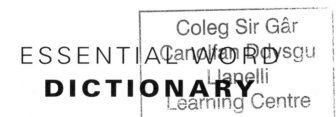

ESSENTIAL WORD
DICTIONARY

For Clare, Adele and Felicity

Philip Allan Updates, part of the Hodder Education Group, an Hachette Livre UK company, Market Place, Deddington, Oxfordshire OX15 0SE

Orders
Bookpoint Ltd, 130 Milton Park, Abingdon, Oxfordshire OX14 4SB
tel: 01235 827720
fax: 01235 400454
e-mail: uk.orders@bookpoint.co.uk
Lines are open 9.00 a.m.–5.00 p.m., Monday to Saturday, with a 24-hour message answering service. You can also order through the Philip Allan Updates website: www.philipallan.co.uk

© Philip Allan Updates 2007

ISBN 978-0-86003-385-1

First printed 2007
Impression number   5   4   3   2   1
Year   2012   2011   2010   2009   2008   2007

Printed in Malta

Philip Allan Updates' policy is to use papers that are natural, renewable and recyclable products and made from wood grown in sustainable forests. The logging and manufacturing processes are expected to conform to the environmental regulations of the country of origin.

P01074

Introduction

This is a dictionary of words and phrases used in the A2 modules in A-level specifications on the government and politics of the USA. For this reason, the definitions are in some cases broader and in others narrower than they would be for the ordinary usage of these words and phrases. The dictionary is not intended as a substitute for a textbook but the definitions are developed, in short accompanying paragraphs, to give further explanations and useful examples. The most up-to-date and pertinent examples at the time of writing have been included although, due to the nature of the subject, many of these will be superseded. Also included are a number of tips to highlight common misunderstandings, comparisons with other political systems and additional points of interest. Throughout the dictionary there are *italicised cross-references* to words and phrases defined elsewhere, which contribute to a more complete understanding of an entry's meaning.

Acknowledgements
Thanks are due to Eric Magee for all his guidance and support over recent years, and also to former colleagues and students at Leicester Grammar School where I spent 10 happy years teaching between 1997 and 2007.

Paul Fairclough

AAA: see *Agricultural Adjustment Act.*

AARP: see *American Association of Retired Persons.*

ABA: see *American Bar Association.*

***Abington v Schempp* (1963):** a case in which the US *Supreme Court* ruled that a state could not require a public school to hold a daily bible reading even if it allowed parents to make a written request for an exemption.

● A Pennsylvania law said that each day had to start with a minimum of ten verses read from the bible. The Schempp family felt that they should not have to request an exemption from a service that they regarded as a violation of the *First Amendment.* They took the case against the Abington School district on behalf of their child who attended Abington High School. The Court struck down the Pennsylvania statute, concluding that it violated the Establishment Clause.

▓ *TIP* This case was crucial in reinforcing the position taken by the Court in earlier rulings, e.g. *Engel v Vitale (1962).*

abortion: in the absence of any explicit reference to abortion in the *Constitution,* the practice was entirely regulated by state governments — under the *Tenth Amendment* — until the landmark *Roe v Wade* case (1973).

● Before *Roe*, Louisiana, New Hampshire and Pennsylvania prohibited abortion in all cases and 29 states permitted abortion only to preserve the woman's life. Only Alaska, DC, Hawaii, New York and Washington State left abortion unrestricted.

● Since the *Roe* ruling prevented states from banning abortion, the debate has polarised. According to Arlen Spector, abortion is now 'the most divisive issue [in America] since slavery'. The debate over *partial birth abortion* has been particularly heated.

● Since 1992 both the *Democratic Party* and the *Republican Party* have had clear statements in their *party platforms*; Democrats *pro-choice* and Republicans *pro-life.*

acceptance speech: the televised address given by the selected presidential candidate on the last day of his or her party's national nominating convention.

- Set-piece events such as the acceptance speech are important because a candidate who performs well can benefit from an immediate bounce in the *opinion polls*.

▨ *e.g.* In 2004, Democrat *John Kerry* alluded to his military record by announcing that he was 'ready for duty' whereas Republican incumbent *George W. Bush* concluded that 'you may not always agree with me, but you know where I stand'.

▨ *COMPARATIVE* In the UK, a party leader's keynote speech at the annual party conference has taken on a similar significance. Candidates who perform badly, for example the Conservative's Iain Duncan Smith, often face opposition within their parties.

accountability: the notion that politicians should be answerable for their actions, either to other elected bodies or directly to the *electorate*.

- The *entrenched separation of powers* present in the US system, allied to the complex system of *checks and balances* means that the *president* is directly accountable to *Congress*.

- House Members are particularly accountable to voters through their biennial elections.

▨ *e.g.* *Bill Clinton* was impeached by the *House of Representatives* for perjury over the *Monica Lewinsky* affair.

▨ *COMPARATIVE* Some argue that committees of all types in the UK Parliament find it harder to hold the *executive* to account due to the fact that their powers of *oversight* are less extensive than those afforded to their US counterparts.

ACLU: see *American Civil Liberties Union*.

ADA: see *Americans for Democratic Action*.

Adams, John (1735–1826): the second US *president*, 1797–1801.

- Adams served as *vice-president* under *George Washington* between 1789 and 1797, having received the second highest number of *Electoral College* votes in the election of 1789. See *Twelfth Amendment (1804)*.

- Adams (a Federalist) defeated *Thomas Jefferson* (a Democratic Republican) by 71 Electoral College votes to 68 in the 1796 presidential election. He was the first US president to occupy the White House.

Adams, John Quincy (1767–1848): the sixth US *president*, 1825–29.

- Adams (a Federalist) was elected in 1824 as the result of a hung *Electoral College*. *Andrew Jackson* had won more Electoral College votes than Adams (99 to 84) but neither won the overall majority required due to the presence of two other candidates.

- Adams won the vote in the House with the support of 13 out of 24 states.

Adarand Constructors v Peña (1995): a case in which the *Supreme Court* struck down a federal government *affirmative action* statute (5:4).

- The federal statute in question gave building contractors bonuses if they took on sub-contractors who employed minority workers.

■ *TIP* The Adarand case was controversial because it appeared to send a broader signal about the way in which the Court would view challenges to other such affirmative action statutes, even though the Court had stopped short of declaring all such programmes *unconstitutional*.

affirmative action: any policy that discriminates positively in favour of a group or groups who have previously been underrepresented — most often discriminated against — in a particular field.

● It most often involves the use of *quotas* as a means of ensuring that different ethnic and social groups are represented in broad proportion to their number in the wider population.

● It provokes strong emotions because the act of discriminating in favour of one group inevitably involves discriminating against others.

■ *e.g.* In the USA, affirmative action programmes in some states once set quotas for the numbers of ethnic minority students who should be admitted to universities. Students in such groups were given more achievable entry grades.

■ *COMPARATIVE* In the UK, Tony Blair's New Labour government sought to make it easier for UK universities to assess the socioeconomic background of prospective students. Some saw this as a way of allowing universities to discriminate in favour of the more economically disadvantaged.

AFL-CIO: see *American Federation of Labor-Congress of Industrial Organisations*.

African-Americans: now referred to more commonly as black Americans. Most often those who are descendants of people brought to the Americas as part of the trade in slaves.

● Many black Americans were involved in the Civil Rights movement of the 1950s and 1960s (see *NAACP* and *Civil Rights Act*).

● Not all Black Americans are descendants of slaves.

■ *e.g.* The black US politician *Barack Obama* was born to a white mother and a Kenyan father. In 2007 it was revealed that some of Obama's ancestors had themselves owned slaves.

agency capture: said to have occurred when a special *interest group* is able to exert a degree of control over the government agency that should be overseeing or regulating the area of policy with which the group is concerned. Once in such a position, the group can often exclude other interested parties from the process of making and administering policy.

● Agency capture is closely linked to the formation of *iron triangles*.

■ *TIP* Agency capture is made easier by the regularity with which individuals working in government agencies move to consultancy positions within companies and other interest groups, and vice versa (see *revolving-door syndrome*).

agenda-setting: the process by which the broad direction of government policy is established and controlled by the adding or subtracting of individual *initiatives*.

- Many argue that the mass *media* has a key role in agenda-setting; forcing the government to pursue a particular course of action. Others see agenda-setting as a function of a ruling elite (see *elites theory*).
- **e.g.** Some argue that powerful groups within the Bush administration were successful in forcing the invasions of Afghanistan and Iraq in the wake of the attacks on *9/11*.
- **COMPARATIVE** In the UK, the popular media's reaction to the Dunblane massacre and the Snowdrop Campaign that followed was widely seen as having forced the government to prioritise the blanket ban on handguns.

Agnew, Spiro (1918–96): *vice-president* (Republican) between 1969 and 1973, having been elected as *Nixon*'s *running mate* in 1968.
- Agnew resigned in 1973 over allegations of corruption during his years in *Maryland* politics. He was replaced by *Gerald Ford*.

Agricultural Adjustment Act (AAA) (1933): part of *Franklin D. Roosevelt*'s *New Deal* programme, this Act was aimed at stabilising prices for farmers.
- Farmers were offered subsidies to cultivate less land.
- This reduction in the area of land cultivated limited the size of the crop surplus, thereby guaranteeing farmers a better price for their produce.
- The AAA, overseen by the Agricultural Adjustment Administration, also resulted in a policy of the deliberate destruction of crops as a means of bringing about a more speedy reduction in the size of the surplus.
- **COMPARATIVE** The subsidies given to farmers for reducing the area of cultivated land can be compared to the policy of set-aside in the EU.

aides: commonly referring to the *president*'s closest advisors, many of whom work in the White House Office.
- **e.g.** One key aide is a president's *chief of staff.*
- **COMPARATIVE** In the UK, it is more common to use the phrase 'special advisor'.

Alabama: the twenty-second state; admitted to the *Union* in 1819.
- Alabama left the *Union* in 1861 when it joined the *Confederacy*. It was readmitted in 1868.
- Birmingham, the largest city in Alabama, was a major focus for the activities of the Black Civil Rights movement in the 1950s and 1960s.

Alaska: the forty-ninth state; admitted to the *Union* in 1959.
- The area of land that became Alaska was purchased from Imperial Russia in 1867.
- Alaska is one of only two US states (the other being Hawaii) that does not share a border with another state.
- It is one of the smallest states in terms of population but it is geographically large. As a result, it has a population density of only 1.1 person per square mile.

***Alexander v Holmes County Board of Education* (1969):** following on in the wake of *Brown v Board of Education (1954)*, this was a case in which the US

Supreme Court ruled that schools should be desegregated at once. See also *Swann* v *Charlotte-Mecklenberg Board of Education (1971).*

Alito, Samuel (1950–): US *Supreme Court* justice appointed in 2006. He was nominated by *George W. Bush* and confirmed by the US *Senate*, 58:42.

- Alito replaced *Sandra Day O'Connor*. O'Connor had been nominated by *Ronald Reagan* as a conservative but was seen as one of the Court's more moderate voices by the time of her retirement.
- O'Connor had often been the key 'swing vote' in decisions where the Court was split 5:4.
- Many felt that the appointment of a conservative such as Alito would alter the balance of the Court and result in more conservative rulings on issues such as *abortion.*

■ *TIP* Conservative justices such as Samuel Alito are often referred to as *strict constructionists* because they tend to interpret the US *Constitution* literally.

Allegheny County v ACLU (1989): a case in which the US *Supreme Court* was asked to rule on whether or not two festive displays violated the Establishment Clause of the *First Amendment.*

- The first, a display in a crèche facility, which involved a manger carrying a crest of an angel holding a banner proclaiming *Gloria in Excelsis Deo*, was declared in violation of the Establishment Clause.
- The second, a large menorah (a symbol of Judaism) positioned next to a Christmas tree accompanied by a sign offering 'festive' as opposed to 'religious' greetings, was considered acceptable under the Clause.

AMA: see *American Medical Association.*

amending the US Constitution: the US *Constitution* is a *codified, entrenched* document. Changes can only be made through a difficult two-stage process.

- Formal proposals for constitutional amendments can be made by means of a super majority of at least two-thirds of each of the two Houses of *Congress* or by a National Constitutional Convention called by two-thirds of states. The latter method has never been used.
- Once a proposal has been formalised in this way it must be ratified by three-quarters of state legislatures or by constitutional conventions in three-quarters of states. The latter method was only used in the case of the *Twenty-First Amendment* (1933).
- There were only 27 amendments to the US Constitution between 1789 and 2007. 10 of those were ratified in 1791 as the *Bill of Rights*. Two of the remaining 15 amendments, the *Eighteenth* and the *Twenty-First,* cancelled one another out by first introducing and then ending Prohibition.

■ *e.g.* Proposed amendments outlawing flag burning and banning same-sex marriage have failed to get past the first stage in recent years. The *Equal Rights Amendment* secured the necessary congressional backing but failed to gain the support of three-quarters of states (38) within the allotted time.

a

■ *TIP* It is often argued that the tortuous amendment process makes the US Constitution rigid. In reality a degree of flexibility is provided by the process of judicial interpretation.

American Association of Retired Persons (AARP): AARP, as it is now known, is a *pressure group* that represents the over-50s.

- In 2007, AARP's membership was said to be in excess of 35 million. Demographic changes mean that this figure could double in the next two decades.

- AARP is a non-profit organisation. It provides a range of products for its members (e.g. insurance) as well as *lobbying* for changes that will benefit the over-50s.

- Some have argued that the ARRP faces a conflict of interests when dealing with public healthcare provision because it has to balance the needs of many of its members against the commercial interests it has in selling related insurance products.

American Bar Association (ABA): a voluntary association of lawyers that plays a major role in establishing required standards at US law schools. It is a respected sectional or *interest group* that speaks on behalf of those in legal practice.

- The ABA is best known for the ratings (ranging from 'not qualified' to 'well qualified') that it gives nominees for posts in the federal *judiciary*.

- In 2001 *George W. Bush* announced that he would no longer be placing any weight on the ABA's ratings when considering nominations to judicial posts. Bush, in common with many on the right, argued that the ABA had an inherent liberal bias and gave unfairly low ratings to conservative nominees.

■ *e.g.* George W. Bush's *Supreme Court* appointees *John Roberts* (2005) and *Samuel Alito* (2006) were both rated 'well qualified'.

American Civil Liberties Union (ACLU): a high profile non-profit *pressure group* that campaigns to protect the individual rights and liberties established under the US *Constitution*.

- The ACLU has been particularly active in the courts, both in bringing its own suits and in submitting *amicus curiae* briefs.

■ *e.g.* In *American Civil Liberties Union* v *Ashcroft (2004)* the ACLU challenged the government's use of wire-taps and other anti-terrorist measures.

■ *TIP* The ACLU is a good example of the way in which US pressure groups hold the government to account.

American Dream: the ideal that any American, regardless of birth, can aspire to achieve any position within society that their abilities merit. This ideal holds that though the individual is owed nothing by the state, few barriers are put in the way of a hard-working, able citizen who is willing to have a go and take the chances that present themselves.

- The American Dream is summed up in the belief that any American can go 'from the log cabin to the White House'.

■ *e.g.* The notion of a citizen progressing from the log cabin to the White House is embodied in *Abraham Lincoln*. In more recent times, successful self-made men such as *Ross Perot* have often been seen as examples of the equality of opportunity in the USA.

■ *TIP* A belief in the American Dream fits in with the notion that the United States is a *pluralist democracy*, though it runs contrary to the central tenets of *elites theory*.

American Federation of Labor-Congress of Industrial Organisations (AFL-CIO): formed in 1955 with the merger of the AFL and the CIO, this is the largest federation of *unions* in the United States.

● A split in 2005 saw a number of larger unions break away from the AFL-CIO. Until that point the organisation represented nearly all unionised workers in the USA.

■ *COMPARATIVE* A UK equivalent to the AFL-CIO would be the Trades Union Congress (TUC).

American Independent Party: originating in California, one of a number of minor political parties that has operated within the US system.

● Regarded as being on the right of the political spectrum, the party campaigned against the *Civil Rights Act (1964)*.

■ *e.g.* The party is most famous for Alabama Governor *George Wallace*'s independent challenge in the 1968 presidential election. Wallace secured 13.5% of the vote nationally and did particularly well in the South, where he won five states and also secured the support of a *rogue elector*. In total Wallace received 46 *Electoral College* votes.

American Medical Association (AMA): the largest association of US doctors; a sectional *pressure group* (interest group) that also seeks to promote the broader cause of improved public health.

American War of Independence: the war through which the 13 American colonies secured their independence from Britain; it is often referred to as the American Revolution.

● Fighting started in 1775, though the war is often dated from the *Declaration of Independence* in 1776.

● American independence was finally confirmed in the Treaty of Paris (1783).

■ *TIP* It is important to remember that the *Founding Fathers* did not meet at Philadelphia to draft the US *Constitution* until 1787. The period between independence and the establishment of the USA saw the former colonies persist with the looser, confederal system of government established under the *Articles of Confederation* (1781).

Americans for Democratic Action (ADA): a liberal-leaning political organisation that has played a key role in advancing civil rights, women's rights and other causes through research, *lobbying* and electioneering.

● Probably best known for its ratings (rankings) of *Congressmen*, which are based upon the degree to which individual legislators' voting records are in line with ADA positions.

a

■ *TIP* Groups that monitor and make public the voting records of legislators play a key role in allowing voters to make informed decisions at the polls. Some argue, however, that such activities lead to electoral witch-hunts.

amicus curiae: groups with a direct interest in a given legal case can file *amicus curiae* (friend of the court) briefs to support their position before legal argument is heard by the court.

● The *NAACP* has often offered such briefs in civil rights cases, as have *pro-life* groups in cases relating to *abortion*.

■ *e.g.* In *Mapp* v *Ohio* (1961) the *ACLU* filed an *amicus curiae* brief that argued that evidence seized without a search warrant should be excluded from a trial.

■ *TIP* Many groups move beyond providing *amicus curiae* briefs to actually sponsoring or even bringing their own cases. The NAACP, for example, sponsored the *Brown* v *Board of Education* case in 1954.

Anderson, John (1922–): once a Republican member of the *House of Representatives*, he was a moderate conservative who ran in the 1980 Republican *presidential primaries* before dropping out and launching an independent candidacy.

● Anderson secured 6.6% of the vote in the presidential election against the Republican candidate *Ronald Reagan* (the eventual winner) and the incumbent Democratic President *Jimmy Carter*.

● Much of Anderson's early support came from the moderate 'Rockefeller Republicans', who regarded Reagan as too extreme.

antebellum: that which occurred before a particular war. In US history the word is most commonly used as part of the phrase 'antebellum south' which refers to the practices common in southern states before the American *Civil War*.

anti-federalists: a movement in the 1780s that argued for the retention of the *Articles of Confederation* and a rejection of the stronger central (federal) government, which was proposed under the new *Constitution* agreed at Philadelphia.

appellate jurisdiction: the *authority* of a court to hear and adjudicate on cases brought on appeal from an inferior court.

● The US *Supreme Court* is the highest court of appeal in the United States.

● It also has the right to hear certain cases for the first time; this is referred to as its original jurisdiction.

■ *TIP* Many US states have their own Supreme Court that acts as the highest appellate court within the state jurisdiction. Many US Supreme Court cases start as appeals resulting from cases in such courts.

■ *e.g.* In the case *George W. Bush et al* v *Albert Gore JR. et al (2000)* the US Supreme Court ruled that the Florida Supreme Court's decision to order the completion of recounts in the presidential election was wrong, both under Florida State law and the *Fourteenth Amendment*.

■ *COMPARATIVE* In the UK, the highest court of appeal has traditionally been the House of Lords. The Constitutional Reform Act of 2005 put in place a timetable under which this power was to be transferred to a new UK Supreme Court.

Appropriations Committee (House and Senate): these committees deal with any bill that authorises the federal spending needed to execute approved government programmes.

- The committees hear testimony and ultimately decide the extent to which government programmes are funded.
- They are an important part of *Congress*'s 'power of the purse'.

Arizona: the forty-eighth state and last of the contiguous states to join the *Union*; admitted in 1912.

- Arizona borders New Mexico, Utah, Nevada and California. It touches corners with Colorado.
- Immigration from Central America and demographic trends within the state suggest that Arizona will be a *majority-minority state* by 2035.

Arkansas: the twenty-fifth state; admitted to the *Union* in 1836.

- *Bill Clinton* was born in Hope, Arkansas and went on to become the state's governor for 12 years (1979–81 and 1983–92) before being elected US *president* in November 1992.

Articles of Confederation: effectively the 'constitution' of the United States between 1781 and 1788.

- The Articles established a loose *confederacy.*
- There was no national *executive* (i.e. no *president*) nor any national *judiciary.* There was simply a *Congress* consisting of representatives from each state. This Congress only had power in respect of foreign policy and defence, territorial disputes between states, coinage, weights and measures, postal services and relations with Indians. All other matters were left to individual states.

▨ *TIP* The federal system adopted by the *Founding Fathers* at Philadelphia is often seen as being a mid-way point between the centralised unitary form of government experienced under British rule and the loose confederacy in operation under the Articles of Confederation.

Ashcroft, John (1942–): a former governor of Missouri and US Senator who went on to serve under *George W. Bush* as US attorney general between 2001 and 2005.

- Regarded as an evangelical conservative on social issues — particularly on issues of race, *abortion* and homosexuality.

***Ashcroft v Free Speech Coalition* (2002):** a case in which the US *Supreme Court* declared the Child Pornography Protection Act (1996) *unconstitutional* because it violated the *First Amendment* protection of free speech.

- The Act had attempted to criminalise the sale, possession or distribution of virtual child pornography, artificially produced images that appeared to show children engaged in sexually explicit conduct.
- It was struck down because the Court argued that it was 'too widely drawn'.

a

■ *e.g.* Justice Kennedy wondered whether mainstream Hollywood films such as *American Beauty* would have been allowed under the Act as it was written. More edgy pieces, such as adaptations of Victor Nabokov's *Lolita* would almost certainly have fallen foul of the Act.

Atkins v Virginia (2002): a case in which the US *Supreme Court* ruled that the execution of mentally retarded criminals violated the *Eighth Amendment*'s prohibition of 'cruel and unusual punishment'. See also *Furman v Georgia (1972)* and *Roper v Simmons (2005)*.

attack-ad: political advertisement that seeks to attack one's opponent rather than advancing a positive message. Such ads are common during the quadrennial presidential election campaign.

■ *e.g.* George Bush senior's 1988 *Willie Horton* ad targeted Democrat opponent *Michael Dukakis*'s record on prisoner release during his time as governor of Massachusetts.

■ *TIP* In the past, attack-ads were sometimes paid for and produced by *interest groups* rather than by the candidates themselves. See *issue advocacy*.

■ *COMPARATIVE* In the UK, political parties are not permitted to buy up advertising slots on commercial television stations.

authority: the right to govern. The authority of democratic governments is said to rest on the fact that they are elected, thus providing them an electoral *mandate.*

● German sociologist Max Weber distinguished between three broad types of authority: traditional authority (relying heavily upon deference); rational-legal authority (rooted in the idea that the people have handed the government power through free and fair elections); and charismatic authority (relying upon the leader's ability to make people want to follow him or her).

■ *TIP* It is important to be able to distinguish between authority (the right to govern) and *power* (the ability to make things happen). Authority can exist without much or indeed any real power.

■ *e.g.* The US *Supreme Court* is a good example of an institution that has great authority but little real power.

Baker, James (1930–): *chief of staff* in *Ronald Reagan*'s first administration (1981–85) before taking on the role of Treasury secretary during Reagan's second term. Baker took on the role of secretary of state under *George H. W. Bush.*

- In 2006, Baker was co-chair of the Iraq Study Group, a high level panel of respected statesmen that was expected to come up with radical solutions to the deteriorating situation in Iraq.
- Baker's fellow co-chair was former Democratic House Member Lee H. Hamilton. As a result the grouping was commonly known as the Baker–Hamilton Iraq Study Group.

***Baker* v *Carr* (1962):** a case in which the US *Supreme Court* ruled that a state's failure to provide equal electoral *districts*, in terms of population, was in violation of the *Fourteenth Amendment*'s guarantee of 'equal protection under the law'.

- This case was the first of a series of rulings that culminated in *Reynolds* v *Sims* (1964). The cumulative effect of such cases has resulted in regular reapportionment of state electoral districts.
- ■ *TIP* It is helpful to make the connection between this legitimate reapportionment — which the Supreme Court has required under the equal protection clause of the Fourteenth Amendment — and *gerrymandering*, which the Court has outlawed using the same passage.

Balanced Budget Amendment: an attempt to amend the US *Constitution* in such a way as to require the incumbent administration to balance spending against incoming revenues.

- Introduced to *Congress* as a proposed constitutional amendment three times between 1995 and 1997, the measure failed to achieve the necessary two-thirds majority in both chambers on all three occasions.
- ■ *e.g.* In 1995, the proposed amendment achieved the two-thirds majority in the *House of Representatives* but failed to do so in the *Senate* and was lost as a result.

■ *TIP* The Balanced Budget Amendment was a product of the *Contract with America platform* that House Speaker *Newt Gingrich*'s Republicans had adopted ahead of the 1994 *mid-term elections*.

balanced ticket: the notion that US parties should try to choose presidential and vice-presidential candidates who appeal to different sections of the US *electorate*.

● This may involve pairing a southern candidate with one from the North, or an older, more experienced candidate with one who is less experienced but more energetic.

■ *e.g.* Many see the Kennedy–Johnson Democratic ticket of 1960 as being a good example of a balanced ticket in terms of experience, age and geographical appeal.

■ *TIP* Though much of the Democrats' support now comes from the northeast and the west coast, it has often been said that Democratic tickets prosper when they have a southerner on the ticket.

band-wagon effect: where favourable poll ratings, or success in the early primary contests in presidential election years, can result in even more voters backing the party or candidate that appears to be 'winning'.

■ *e.g.* The way in which *John Kerry* was able to build up a momentum that saw him effectively secure the Democratic nomination by early March 2004.

■ *TIP* In the USA, band-wagons are often closely associated with the *coat-tails effect*, where candidates for *Congress* representing the same party as a victorious presidential candidate are swept into power on his 'coat-tails' — a form of reflected glory.

base-line poll: a poll that is taken ahead of an election as a means of gauging the public mood.

● Baseline polls are used by political consultants as a means of framing a candidate's campaign around the issues that have resonance with voters.

● *Tracking polls* are then conducted at regular intervals during the campaign in order to assess the effectiveness of the campaign and to refocus the candidate's message where new issues have come to the fore.

BCRA: see *Bipartisan Campaign Finance Reform Act (2002)*.

Bernstein, Carl (1944–): see *Woodward, Bob*.

Bible Belt: those states in which various forms of evangelical Protestantism (e.g. Southern Baptism) are at the heart of everyday life.

● The term was coined in the 1920s by journalist H. L. Mencken.

● The Belt has traditionally encompassed all of the South as well as a number of adjacent states.

bicameral: a term commonly used to refer to those *legislatures* that have two distinct chambers.

● The US *Congress* is a bicameral legislature consisting of the *House of Representatives* and the *Senate*.

- Forty-nine US states also had bicameral legislatures in 2007. The fiftieth, *Nebraska*, has adopted a unicameral model.
- **TIP** In many bicameral US state legislatures the lower chamber is called the Assembly and the upper is the Senate.
- **COMPARATIVE** One proposed model for parliamentary reform in the UK would have seen the move towards a unicameral legislative model with the outright abolition of the Lords.

Bill of Rights: a collective term referring to the first ten amendments to the US *Constitution*.

- The Bill of Rights was ratified in 1791.
- It is commonly seen as part of a package of concessions that persuaded some states to ratify the Constitution itself.
- **e.g.** The *First Amendment* protects the freedom of religion, the press, speech and assembly.
- **TIP** It is important to remember that although many of the protected rights appear unambiguous and clear cut (absolute), in reality the *Supreme Court* and inferior courts have had to balance the rights of one individual against another and balance the rights of all individuals against the legitimate interests of the state in regulating human activity.
- **COMPARATIVE** In the UK the term Bill of Rights refers to a statute passed in 1689 that placed some restrictions on the power of the monarch, identified some key parliamentary powers and certain individual rights. It is more common to compare the UK's Human Rights Act (1998) with the US Bill of Rights.

Bipartisan Campaign Finance Reform Act (BCRA) (2002): introduced amidst ongoing concerns regarding the activity of *political action committees* and the growth in *soft money*, this Act sought to amend some of the regulations contained in the Federal Election Campaign Acts of the 1970s.

- The Act introduced an outright ban on soft money.
- It increased the $1,000 limit on individual donations, established by the *Federal Election Campaign Act (1974)*, to $2,000.
- It restricted the use of electioneering ads by companies, corporations or *unions* featuring the likenesses or names of candidates within 30 days of a *primary election* or 60 days of a general election.
- **TIP** The Act's major provisions were upheld in *McConnell* v *Federal Electoral Commission (2003)*.
- **COMPARATIVE** UK parallels could be drawn with the passage of the Political Parties, Elections and Referendum Act (2000) and with the Philips Report (2007).

bipartisanship: said to be in evidence where the two parties cooperate on areas of common cause as opposed to defaulting to positions that are mutually antagonistic.

■ *e.g.* In the wake of *Democratic Party* success in the 2006 *mid-term elections* it was said that *George W. Bush* and the Republicans in *Congress* might look to build bipartisan coalitions on issues such as immigration and Iraq.

■ *TIP* With divided government, the absence of bipartisanship can result in legislative gridlock.

Board of Education v Earls (2002): a case in which the US *Supreme Court* found that students attending an after-school programme in Oklahoma could be legally required to undergo a random drug test.

● The Court ruled (5:4) that the test had not violated the *Fourth Amendment*'s prohibition of 'unreasonable searches and seizures'.

boomerang effect: where strong *opinion poll* ratings for one party result in some of its supporters not bothering to vote whilst at the same time more of the trailing party's supporters are encouraged to turn out, the result being that the gap identified by the poll closes.

● The boomerang effect can be contrasted with the *band-wagon effect*.

■ *COMPARATIVE* The tendency of opinion polls to influence as opposed to simply reflecting the public mood has resulted in some countries (France, for example) restricting their use or even banning them in the weeks immediately preceding elections.

Bork, Robert (1927–): a conservative lawyer and legal scholar who was nominated to the *Supreme Court* by *Ronald Reagan* in 1987, but rejected by the US *Senate*.

● Bork was nominated as a replacement for Lewis Powell, who resigned in 1987. Powell had often been the crucial swing-vote in the Court on matters concerning civil rights. The Democrat-controlled Senate feared that the appointment of the conservative Bork would fundamentally change the balance of the Court.

● The Senate rejected Bork's nomination by 58 votes to 42, despite his considerable legal experience.

■ *TIP* Bork was well aware of the motivations of many of those who voted against his nomination. As he later wrote, 'the Constitution is...power. That is why we see political struggle over the selection of judges who will wield that power'.

Bradley, Bill (1943–): a former basketball player and US Senator who challenged *Vice-President Al Gore* for the Democratic nomination in the 2000 presidential election.

● Though he performed creditably in the *New Hampshire primary*, securing 70,502 votes to Gore's 76,897, Bradley's challenge faded thereafter — partly due to a lack of campaign finance.

Brady Bill: this bill initially required a waiting period of up to 5 days when buying a handgun in order for the completion of background checks on the purchaser.

● The Act was named after James Brady, a policy officer shot and injured during the attempted assassination of *Ronald Reagan* in 1981.

■ *TIP* The measure ran into entrenched opposition from the *National Rifle Association* and also faced *Supreme Court* challenges under the *Second Amendment*.

■ *COMPARATIVE* In the UK, the government had little difficulty in passing a ban on handguns in the wake of the Dunblane Massacre. This is because the UK does not have an *entrenched* constitutional guarantee of the right to bear arms along the lines of the Second Amendment to the US *Constitution*.

Branch Davidians: a religious group that emerged from a sect who were originally part of the Seventh Day Adventist Church.

● Notable for the 1993 siege of their compound at Waco, Texas, by agents of the Federal Bureau of Investigations (FBI) and the Bureau of Alcohol, Tobacco and Firearms (ATF), which resulted in the death of 82 members of the group, including their leader David Koresh.

Brennan, William J. (1906–97): a *Supreme Court* justice nominated by President *Dwight Eisenhower* in 1956, who served on the Court until his retirement in 1990.

● Brennan is widely regarded as one of the most influential liberal-leaning justices in the Court's history.

Breyer, Stephen (1938–): a *Supreme Court* justice nominated by President *Bill Clinton* in 1994. He is generally regarded as one of the more liberal members of the Court.

Brownlow Committee: formally the President's Committee on Administrative Management, the Brownlow Committee produced the 1937 Brownlow Report, which recommended sweeping changes in the organisation of the US *executive*.

● The committee concluded that 'the President needs help'.

● Its recommendations led to the emergence of the *Executive Office of the President (EXOP)*.

Brown v Board of Education of Topeka (1954): a case in which the US *Supreme Court* ruled that racial segregation in schools violated the 'equal protection under the law' afforded by the *Fourteenth Amendment*.

● In *Plessy v Ferguson (1896)* the Court had allowed segregated trains, concluding that races could be 'separate but equal' thus circumventing the Fourteenth Amendment.

● In *Brown* the Court used new sociological research to show that segregation inevitably created inequalities and was, therefore, *unconstitutional*.

■ *TIP* The *Brown* case effectively set a *precedent* that could be applied to segregation in all areas of life.

Buchanan, James (1791–1868): the fifteenth US *president*, 1857–61.

● Regarded as a weak president because he appeared to lack the conviction to tackle the secession of the southern states, a move which he acknowledged was illegal. His inaction was in sharp contrast to the decisive action of his successor in the White House — *Abraham Lincoln*.

b

Buchanan, Patrick (1938–): a successful author and broadcaster, he was a candidate for the Republican nomination in the presidential elections of 1992 and 1996 and the *Reform Party* candidate in the 2000 presidential election.

- The bitterness of the 1992 Republican nomination contest between Buchanan and incumbent president *George H. W. Bush,* which spilled over into the Republicans' national convention, was said to have contributed to *Bill Clinton's* victory in the presidential election proper.

Buckley v Valeo (1976): a case in which the US *Supreme Court* ruled on the constitutionality of some of the campaign finance regulations brought in under the *Federal Election Campaign Act* of 1974 (FECA 1974).

- The Court upheld the FECA limits on campaign contributions but also recognised that spending money in order to influence the outcome of elections is a form of free speech (expressive conduct) protected under the *First Amendment.*
- The Court ruled that a candidate's spending on their own campaign was not subject to limits.

budget: see *federal budget.*

Budget and Impoundment Control Act (1974): an Act that sought to set out more clearly the role of *Congress* in the budgetary process and regulate the practice of *impoundment.*

- One of the main provisions of the Act prevented the *president* from impounding funds that had been approved to fund government programmes, unless he could get congressional support for such a move.
- The Act was seen as a response to President *Nixon's* use of impoundment as a means of blocking those programmes of which he disapproved.

■ *TIP* Alongside the *Case Act (1972)* and the *War Powers Act (1973)* the Budget and Impoundment Control Act is often seen as part of a 1970s congressional fight-back.

building up the base (or energising the base)**:** the practice of targeting one's own natural supporters in an election campaign in order to ensure that they register, turn out and vote in line with their party allegiance.

- A tactic closely associated with *George W. Bush's* chief campaign advisor *Karl Rove* in 2004.

■ *TIP* Often seen as a more effective campaign strategy when the numbers of voters identifying with each of the major parties is such that victory can be secured by getting one's own vote out as opposed to attracting independent voters or those who have traditionally supported the opposition.

Burger, Warren Earl (1907–95): chief justice of the US *Supreme Court* between 1969 and 1986 having been nominated by President *Richard Nixon.*

- The Burger Court followed the activist Court of Chief Justice *Earl Warren* and, like its predecessor, delivered a number of constitutionally significant rulings.

■ *e.g.* See *Swann v Charlotte-Mecklenburg Board of Education (1971), Furman v Georgia (1972),* and *Roe v Wade (1973).*

b

Bush, George H. W. (1924–): the forty-first US *president*, 1989–93.

- Bush had served as *vice-president* to *Ronald Reagan* between 1981 and 1989. He had previously been a member of the *House of Representatives* (1967–71) and the director of the CIA (1976–77).
- Bush's success in the First Gulf War (1991) was not enough to carry him to victory in the 1992 presidential election where he was defeated by the *Democratic Party* candidate *Bill Clinton.*

Bush, George W. (1946–): the forty-third US *president*, 2001–09.

- Bush jr. served as governor of Texas for 6 years prior to his inauguration as US president in January, 2001.
- He secured a second term in the 2004 presidential election where he defeated the *Democratic Party* candidate *John Kerry.*
- **TIP** Bush's two terms as president were shaped largely by his response to the attacks that came just 8 months into his first term on *9/11.*

Bush v Gore (2000): a case in which the US *Supreme Court* effectively handed *George W. Bush* victory in the 2000 presidential election by ordering a halt to recounts being conducted in some Florida counties.

- The Court ruled that the lack of a standardised system for conducting recounts across all counties meant that Florida voters were being denied the 'equal protection under the law' guaranteed by the *Fourteenth Amendment.*
- The Florida Supreme Court's earlier ruling that the counts should continue also appeared to violate the state's own election regulations.
- **TIP** Though some critics saw the Court's decision as a political one — motivated by the fact that many of those on the Court had been appointed by Republicans such as *Ronald Reagan* or George W. Bush's own father (*George H. W. Bush*) — the decision was based upon established legal *precedent.*

bussing: the practice of creating a more socially representative ethnic balance within public educational facilities by transporting students of different races between schools in different areas.

- Bussing was introduced in the wake of the US *Supreme Court* case *Swann v Charlotte-Mecklenberg Board of Education (1971).*
- **TIP** Earlier Supreme Court cases (see *Brown v Board of Education*) had sought to end legally enforced (i.e. de jure) segregation. Bussing was one way of dealing with the de facto segregation that had resulted from where concentrations of different ethnic groups had chosen to live.

cabinet: a coordinating committee of the *executive* comprising the *president*, the *vice-president*, the heads of the various *executive departments* (referred to as secretaries) and other leading figures.

- The only elected members of the US cabinet are the president and the vice-president. Members of *Congress* are prevented from holding cabinet offices simultaneously as a result of the *separation of powers*.

■ *TIP* The fact that the US *Constitution* makes no mention of the cabinet means that its form and function remain largely dependent upon the person in whom the Constitution vests all executive power, i.e. the president.

■ *COMPARATIVE* Whereas in Britain, cabinet ministers are invariably generalists who move between departments as a result of reshuffles, US cabinet members are more often specialists in their field.

calendar: the various congressional calendars list the bills, resolutions and other business that is pending.

- Bills are formally placed on a calendar when they are reported out of committee.
- The *House Rules Committee* and the *Senate majority leader* will then decide on the order in which items are drawn from the calendar for action on the floor of each chamber.

California: the thirty-first state; joined the *Union* in 1850.

- California is the largest of the US states by population. In 2007 the state had an estimated population of around 36.5 million.

campaign finance reform: see *Federal Election Campaign Act (1974)* and *Bipartisan Campaign Finance Reform Act (2002)*.

candidate-centred campaigns: contests that are fought on the basis of each candidate's personal qualities and appeal as opposed to party labels, policies, or issues.

- Such campaigns are often said to be a direct consequence of the rise of the modern mass *media* and a greater use of *primary elections* when selecting candidates.

■ *e.g.* The *modus operandi* of former actor and two-term president *Ronald Reagan*, known as 'the great communicator', was said to epitomise such developments.

candidate selection: the processes by which each party's candidates for federal, state and local elections are chosen.

● In most states, candidates were once chosen through a system of *caucuses*. In the modern era, *primary elections* have taken the place of caucuses in most states.

■ *TIP* The rise of primary elections is said to have reduced the influence that US political parties have over the selection of the candidates who stand in their name.

■ *COMPARATIVE* As a result of the rise of primary elections, US parties do not have the powers (e.g. to discipline and ultimately de-select candidates) that are available to their UK counterparts.

capital punishment: commonly referred to as 'the death penalty' and permitted in three-quarters of the 50 US states in 2007. Provision for capital punishment also exists for serious offences at federal level and in cases heard under military jurisdiction.

● Capital punishment was effectively stopped in the USA between 1973 and 1976 following a series of controversial *Supreme Court* cases (see *Furman* v *Georgia*).

■ *e.g.* The Oklahoma bomber Timothy McVeigh was executed in 2001.

■ *COMPARATIVE* The death penalty was abolished in the UK in 1969.

Card, Andrew (1947–): President *George W. Bush*'s *chief of staff* between 2001 and April 2006. Previously the US secretary of transportation under *George H. W. Bush*.

Carswell, Harrold (1919–92): a US District Court judge who was nominated as a US *Supreme Court* justice by *Richard Nixon*. Concerns over his performance on the bench and his record on civil rights resulted in the *Senate* rejecting his nomination, 51:45. See also *Clement Haynesworth*.

Carter, Jimmy (1924–): the thirty-ninth US president. He served from 1977 to 1981 having defeated the incumbent Republican President *Gerald Ford* in the 1976 presidential election.

● A former peanut farmer and governor of Georgia whose election, some argue, owed as much to the public angst following the *Watergate Scandal* as it did to his own personal qualities.

Case Act (1972): a measure that sought to regulate the president's excessive use of *executive agreements*. Such devices were being used as a means of circumventing the two-thirds *Senate* majority required for the *ratification* of formal *treaties*.

● The Case Act required the president to notify *Congress* within 60 days of an executive agreement being made. This gave Congress the opportunity to vote to cancel such agreements or withhold funding, thereby stopping their implementation.

■ *TIP* Though the Act was aimed at limiting the power of the *executive*, it had the effect of granting the president the power to act beyond his *enumerated constitutional powers*.

■ *COMPARATIVE* In the UK, the prime minister can legally make treaties without parliamentary approval. This is because treaty-making is covered by the prerogative powers that the prime minister exercises on behalf of the monarch.

caucus: a meeting of members of a political *party* convened with a view to selecting candidates, deciding policy, or coordinating the party's efforts more generally.

● The term is often used with reference to the meetings that take place in those states who do not use *primary elections* in the quadrennial presidential election.

● Also used to refer to the grouping of each party within *Congress* (e.g. 'the Democratic caucus') or to other groupings of members within Congress (e.g. 'the black caucus').

cause groups: *pressure groups* that seek to promote a particular cause as opposed to bringing direct benefits to their members.

certiorari: in the USA, a legal term commonly referring to a writ issued by the *Supreme Court* to an inferior court announcing its intention to review an earlier judgement for legal error.

● In the absence of an automatic right of appeal, those looking to take cases to the US Supreme Court will petition for a writ of certiorari.

Chao, Elaine (1953–): the first Asian-American woman to serve in the US *cabinet*, Chao held the position of secretary of labor under President *George W. Bush*.

Chappaquiddick: refers to the incident in which a woman travelling in a car driven by US Senator *Edward (Teddy) Kennedy* was drowned when the vehicle in question careered off a bridge and sank.

● Kennedy managed to swim clear of the car and claimed that he had tried to rescue his passenger. Even so, speculation surrounding the incident was said to have influenced the Senator's decision not to run in the 1972 presidential election.

checks and balances: where each branch of the federal government exercises controls over the other branches and is, in turn, controlled by them.

● Best summed up in *Richard Neustadt*'s concept of 'separated institutions, shared powers'.

■ *e.g.* The way in which presidential appointments to the *cabinet*, the US *Supreme Court* and other key positions can only be made with the 'advice and consent of the *Senate*'.

■ *TIP* One should remember that the effectiveness of such checks and balances depends upon the abilities and attitudes of those in office at any given time.

Cheney, Richard 'Dick' (1941–): *vice-president* to *George W. Bush* and also a former *chief of staff*, secretary of defense and member of the *House of Representatives*.

● In addition to his political roles, he was the chief executive officer of Halliburton Energy Services, a company in which he retained a significant shareholding during his time as vice-president.

Chester, Alan Arthur (1829–86): the twenty-first US *president*, 1881–85.

chief of staff: often regarded as the 'gatekeeper' to the *president*, the chief of staff is the highest ranking member of the *Executive Office of the President (EXOP)*.

● The chief of staff organises the work of the *White House Staff* and controls the president's schedule.

▆ *TIP* Though an effective chief of staff will help the president manage the various demands on his time effectively, presidents who rely too heavily on their 'gatekeepers' can lose touch with what is going on outside the Oval Office. See *Bob Haldeman*.

Christian Coalition: an evangelical Christian campaign group founded by the Rev. Pat Robertson in 1989. Seen by many as the natural successor to *Jerry Falwell's Moral Majority*.

***City of Akron v Akron Center for Reproductive Health Inc.* (1983):** a case in which the US *Supreme Court* struck down a number of local statutes which were considered too restrictive of the practice of *abortion*.

Civil Rights Act (1964): an Act of *Congress* that outlawed discrimination on grounds of race, gender, religion and national origin in relation to voting rights, access to public services, and employment.

Civil Rights Act (1968): primarily concerned with extending the *Civil Rights Act (1964)* to cover the sale and rental of housing.

civil servant: an unelected bureaucrat.

● Around 3 million civil servants are employed by the US *federal bureaucracy*.

civil service: often used interchangeably with the term 'federal bureaucracy' in the USA, the unelected part of the government machine.

▆ *TIP* It is worth remembering that the US *cabinet* is technically part of the federal bureaucracy as its members are unelected.

▆ *COMPARATIVE* Many of the *civil servants* who work in the UK and US bureaucracies are not located in their respective capitals but in the various departmental offices, *executive agencies* and other bodies that are located around each country.

Civil Service Reform Act (1978): an Act of *Congress* that transformed the United States Civil Service Commission into the Office of Personnel Management.

● The Act also made it possible for civil servants to be moved into any position within the service for which they were qualified. This change allowed the rank of political appointees at the top of the bureaucracy to assemble teams in their own image.

Civil War (1861–65): a conflict that resulted from the secession of 11 southern states where *slavery* was permitted from the *Union*.

- The secession states formed the Confederate States of America.
- Fighting started in 1861 when Confederate forces attacked federal government forces at Fort Sumter, North Carolina.
- The forces of the Union, led by Republican President *Abraham Lincoln*, rejected the right of the southern states to secede from the Union and eventually emerged victorious over the Confederate forces in 1865.

Clean Air Act: any one of a number of measures passed by *Congress* since the 1960s which have sought to reduce atmospheric pollution.

- *e.g.* the Clean Air Act (1963).

Cleveland, Grover (1837–1908): the twenty-second and twenty-fourth US *president*, 1885–89 and 1893–97.

clientelism: where *executive agencies* come to favour the interests of those that they should be overseeing at the expense of the broader public interest. This is a particular problem in respect of independent regulatory commissions. See *agency capture*.

Clinton, Hillary (1947–): US Senator for New York and former first lady to President *Bill Clinton*. Clinton announced her intention to run for the 2008 Democratic presidential nomination early in 2007.

Clinton v New York City (1998): a case in which the US *Supreme Court* ruled (6:3) that the powers afforded to the US president in the Line Item Veto Act (1996) were *unconstitutional*. See *Line-Item Veto*.

Clinton, William [Bill] J. (1946–): the forty-second US *president*, 1993–2001.

- Clinton's efforts to pass his flagship *healthcare reform* package were thwarted by fellow Democrats in *Congress* during his first 2 years in office.
- The president's aims in domestic policy had to be revised again following the Republican takeover of both houses of Congress following the 1994 *mid-term elections*. Despite this, Clinton was able to achieve a good deal between 1994 and 2001 by focusing on issues where there could be some bipartisan agreement.

- *e.g.* The rejection of Clinton's *budget* in 1995 led to a partial shut-down in Washington.

- *TIP* Clinton was impeached by the House in 1998, in the wake of the *Monica Lewinsky* scandal, but he was acquitted in the *Senate*.

closure [cloture]: see *cloture*.

cloture [closure]: a *Senate* motion that brings a debate to an end, effectively thwarting any attempt to *filibuster* a bill out of time.

- First introduced in 1917 and requiring a two-thirds supermajority, the Senate failed to achieve the majority required for cloture on a number of controversial bills relating to civil rights.

- In 1975 the Democratic majority in the Senate was able to force through a procedural change which reduced the majority required for cloture from two-thirds (i.e. 67) to three-fifths (i.e. 60).
- **TIP** In the last 20 years the use of filibuster tactics as a means of preventing a vote being taken on judicial nominations has brought the majority required for cloture into focus once more.
- **COMPARATIVE** Similar limitations are placed on debate in the UK, though the term guillotine is often used in preference to cloture.

coat-tails effect: where candidates representing the same party as a popular presidential candidate will also prosper when elections are held at the same time. An unpopular presidential candidate might equally bring about a reverse-coat-tails effect.

- **e.g.** Republican successes in the presidential and congressional elections of 2004.
- **TIP** A coat-tails effect could be seen as evidence of '*straight-ticket*' as opposed to '*split-ticket*' voting.

codified constitution: a *constitution* that consists of a full and authoritative set of rules written down in a single place.

- **e.g.** The US Constitution is said to be a codified constitution.
- **COMPARATIVE** The UK is said to have an uncodified constitution. This is because it has evolved over time and become as much reliant on traditions and customs as those written documents that do exist.

Colorado: the thirty-eighth state; joined the *Union* in 1867.

committee chairmen: refers specifically to those individuals who chair *standing committees* within the *House of Representatives* and the *Senate*.

- Chairmen have considerable power over the treatment of bills in committee, including the power to prioritise and *pigeon-hole* bills.
- Those looking to secure safe passage for their bills will often try to secure 'pork' for such chairmen's home states (see *pork-barrelled bill*).

committee hearings: where *standing committees* in the *House* and *Senate* allow witnesses to give evidence as a part of their scrutiny of legislation.

- The committee hearings are similar to trials in format, with evidence being brought forward by specialists and interested parties alike.
- *Pressure groups* with an interest in a particular piece of legislation will send professional *lobbyists* to the committee hearings and to meet the committee members who they feel might be sympathetic to their case.
- **TIP** The belief in hearings stems from the fact that, as Ernest S. Griffith observed, 'truth customarily emerges from a battle of protagonists'.

Committee to Re-elect the President: often shortened to CREEP, a White House-based fundraising organisation that worked on behalf of President *Richard Nixon* in his 1972 re-election campaign.

- The indirect use of CREEP funds to help the Watergate burglars defend themselves in 1972 ultimately led *Washington Post* reporters *Bob Woodward* and *Carl Bernstein* to expose the broader *Watergate scandal*.

Common Cause: founded in 1970 and having around 300,000 members, a non-partisan *lobbying* group that seeks to curb the influence of wealthy *interest groups* and ensure that government is serving the broader public good.

concurrent powers: those powers that are held jointly by both the federal government and the individual states.

- ▦ *e.g.* the power to levy taxes.
- ▦ *TIP* Students should be able to distinguish between *enumerated, reserved*, and concurrent powers.
- ▦ *COMPARATIVE* Under the UK's unitary system, all power is ultimately held by the Parliament at Westminster.

Confederacy: referring to the Confederate States of America, the government formed by the 11 states that seceded from the *Union* in 1861. See *Civil War*.

Conference Committee (Joint-Action Committee): a committee normally comprising members of the relevant *standing committees* in each chamber of *Congress*, convened as a means of resolving differences between the *House* and *Senate* versions of a given bill.

- The need for such committees stems from the fact that the House and the Senate have co-equal legislative power.
- ▦ *COMPARATIVE* In the UK, the House of Commons can use, or threaten to use, the Parliament Act as a means of ensuring that its version of the bill will pass into law, e.g. over the ban on fox hunting. By convention, the Salisbury Doctrine also meant that the Lords were more likely to give way.

Congress (US): a *bicameral legislature* comprising the *House of Representatives* and the *Senate*.

congressional committees: see *standing committees, select committee* and *Conference Committee*.

congressional elections: elections for the *House of Representatives* and for the US *Senate*.

- The House of Representatives is elected in its entirety every 2 years. This means that the whole House is elected in presidential election years but also in mid-term *elections*, 2 years into a presidential term.
- Senators are elected for 6-year terms, but the Senate is divided into three 'classes' or cohorts, with one third of the Senate elected every 2 years.

Congressmen: members of either of the two chambers in the *bicameral* US *legislature*. Often used more loosely to refer to members of the *House of Representatives* alone.

- ▦ *TIP* Referring to members of the House of Representatives as House Members will avoid the confusion that may result from the use of the term Congressmen.

Connecticut: the fifth state; joined the *Union* in 1788.

Connecticut Compromise: proposed by the Connecticut delegate Roger Sherman at the *Philadelphia Convention* of 1787, a means by which the interests of the smaller states could be balanced against those of the larger ones.

- Larger states had supported the *Virginia Plan*, which held that seats in both chambers of the *bicameral* system should be apportioned between states on the basis of population.
- Smaller states were worried that this would see their voice lost in the new *Congress* and were unwilling to agree to a *constitution* that would result in such a situation. They favoured the *New Jersey Plan*, which offered equal representation.
- Sherman's historic compromise offered a solution. One chamber (the *House*) would be apportioned in relation to a state's population and the other (the *Senate*) would comprise two representatives from each state.

Connor, Eugene 'Bull' (1897–1973]: a pro-segregationist police official in Birmingham, Alabama in the 1960s who used police attack dogs and fire hoses against unarmed, non-violent civil rights protestors.

- Ironically, broadcast images of such actions helped to ease the passage of the *Civil Rights Act of 1964* that Connor and his supporters opposed.

constitution: a constitution is a body of rules that defines the manner in which a state or society is organised. It sets out the way in which sovereign power is distributed between the government and the people, and between the government's constituent parts.

- Constitutions can be broadly divided into those that are codified (see *codified constitution*) and those that are not.
- The US Constitution was framed by the *Founding Fathers* who met at the *Philadelphia Constitutional Convention* of 1787. It replaced the *Articles of Confederation*.
- **TIP** A constitution provides a framework upon which more complex rules, structures and processes can be built. Even states with codified constitutions have some of their rules based in regular statute, judicial precedent (common law) and in convention.

constitutional sovereignty: the notion that supreme *authority* rests with the US *Constitution*.

- It is often argued that *sovereignty* in the USA in fact lies with the people as the government was established in their name. This concept of *popular sovereignty* is also linked to the idea of *limited government*.
- Comparative constitutional or popular sovereignty in the USA is normally contrasted with parliamentary sovereignty in the UK.

Continental Congress: the first 'US' government comprising the representatives drawn from the 13 British-owned American colonies.

- The First Continental Congress was established in 1774.

- The Second Continental Congress ran from 1775 until the *ratification* of the *Articles of Confederation* in 1781. This Second Congress was responsible for the *Declaration of Independence* in 1776.

Contract with America: a document amounting to an election manifesto. Issued by the Republicans as part of their campaign in the 1994 *mid-term elections*.

- The Contract was strongly associated with *Newt Gingrich*, the man who became the Republican House Speaker in January 1995 following the party's success in the elections of that year.
- *e.g.* The Contract proposed a number reforms to 'clean up' *Congress* as well as an explicit commitment to a balanced budget.
- *TIP* It is widely seen as evidence of increased *party* coherence and cohesion, within the *legislature* at least.

convention: an accepted rule of constitutional practice that has evolved over time.

- Conventions are not legally enforceable but they have persuasive *authority*.
- *e.g.* The way in which recent presidents, most notably *George W. Bush*, have issued statements (known as *signing statements*) when signing bills approved by *Congress* into law.
- *TIP* It is important to remember that the presence of a *codified constitution* does not rule out the existence of other sources of constitutional law within a given jurisdiction.

Coolidge, Calvin (1872–1933): the thirtieth US *president*, 1923–29.

cooperative federalism: often referred to as intergovernmentalism, a way of describing the style of *federalism* operating in the USA between the 1930s and the 1960s.

- The federal government was forced to become more involved in coordinating efforts to kick-start the US economy in the wake of the *Wall Street Crash* (1929).
- *Franklin D. Roosevelt's New Deal* made the federal government more overtly involved in everyday life. *Truman's* Fair Deal, *Kennedy's New Frontier* and *Johnson's Great Society* continued this interventionist trend, particularly in their use of targeted grants.
- *TIP* It is important to understand that federalism is not a fixed system but an ever-evolving, organic one. Contrast cooperative federalism with the *dual federalism* that preceded it, or the *new federalism* that has emerged since the 1970s.

court-packing: any effort to control the US *Supreme Court* by enlarging it and filling the resulting vacancies with one's own supporters, thus outnumbering opponents already sitting on the bench.

- This is possible with the support of the *executive* and the *legislature* because the size of the Supreme Court is controlled by the US *Congress* and vacancies are filled by the *president* of the day, with the advice and consent of the *Senate*.

■ *e.g.* *Franklin D. Roosevelt* threatened 'court-packing' over the Supreme Court's opposition to some elements of his *New Deal* programme. He suggested adding one additional justice for every existing justice over 70, up to a maximum of six extra justices. Roosevelt's pressure saw the Court back down over the New Deal, though his 'court-packing bill' was not ultimately passed.

cruel and unusual punishment: constitutionally prohibited under the *Eighth Amendment* to the US *Constitution*.

● Those seeking to outlaw *capital punishment* in the USA have often sought to achieve their goal by persuading the *Supreme Court* that such a punishment violates the Eighth Amendment. See *Furman* v *Georgia (1972)*.

Cuban Missile Crisis (1962): a Cold War crisis that saw the US president *John F. Kennedy* and the Soviet premier Nikita Khruschev engaged in a stand-off over the USSR's attempt to site intermediate range nuclear missiles on Cuba.

Davis v Bandemer (1986): a case in which the US *Supreme Court* ruled that whilst *gerrymandering* remained *unconstitutional* under the 'equal protection clause' of the *Fourteenth Amendment,* Indiana had not been guilty of it when reapportioning state *districts.*

DC: see *District of Columbia.*

Dean, Howard (1948–): former governor of Vermont and early front runner in the race for the 2004 Democratic nomination that was eventually won by Senator *John Kerry.* Dean also founded the organisation Democracy for America and was elected chair of the *Democratic National Committee (DNC)* following the party's defeat in the 2004 presidential election.

- Dean put together a vibrant grassroots campaign during the *invisible primary* for the 2004 presidential election. He raised over $50,000,000, mostly in small donations.

- Dean's campaign made extensive use of net-campaigning and online donations in 2004. As chair of the DNC he pioneered a '50-state strategy' that was credited in part with bringing the Democrats success in the 2006 *mid-term elections.*

■ *TIP* Dean's 2004 defeat in the Iowa *caucus* and the reaction to his so-called 'I have a scream' speech that followed that defeat is a good example of the way in which candidates who fail to gain early successes in election year can struggle thereafter.

death penalty: see *capital punishment.*

Declaration of Independence (1776): largely written by *Thomas Jefferson* and adopted by the Second *Continental Congress* in 1776, the statement formally declared that the United Colonies were independent of British rule. The Declaration also set out a theoretical justification for this independence.

Deep South: a phrase that describes a region in the southeast of the United States, commonly said to include some or all of those states that seceded from the *Union* in 1861.

- The Deep South was traditionally associated with *slavery* and segregationist attitudes.

- The region was once a stronghold for the Democrats, a reaction to the Republican President *Abraham Lincoln*'s historic role in defeating the Confederate forces and abolishing slavery.
- **e.g.** The term normally covers Alabama, Louisiana, Mississippi, Florida, North Carolina and South Carolina.
- **TIP** The term can be used in a cultural as well as a geographical sense e.g. 'Deep South values'.

Defense Department: an *executive department* of the US government originally known as the Department of War. It has a broad responsibility for matters concerning the military and issues of national security.

- The Department of War was one of the three original executive departments created in 1789. It became the Department of Defense in 1949.
- The emergence of government agencies (e.g. the CIA) and new government departments (e.g. Homeland Security in 2003) have had an impact on the role of the Defense Department in respect of security.

Delaware: the first state; joined the *Union* in 1787.

Democratic National Committee (DNC): first established in 1848, the national body that oversees the organisation of the *Democratic Party*, organises the *party convention* in presidential election years, and helps to coordinate the party's electoral efforts between presidential elections.

- The DNC is formally elected at the quadrennial national party convention and headed by an elected chair.
- **e.g.** In 2007 the DNC was chaired by failed 2004 Democrat presidential hopeful and former governor of Vermont *Howard Dean*.
- **TIP** Other bodies also play a significant role in devising Democrat campaign strategies, e.g. the Democratic Congressional Campaign Committee (in the House) and the Democratic Senatorial Campaign Committee.

Democratic Party: said to be the oldest political party in the world, it has its roots in the Democratic-Republican Party formed in 1792.

- Over the last 100 years the party has moved to a position that is consistently to the left of the Republicans, particularly on social issues such as welfare provision, *gun control* and access to *abortion*.
- **e.g.** Since the 1992 presidential election the Democratic Party's *platform* has been explicitly *pro-choice* on the issue of abortion.
- **TIP** In the early part of the twentieth century the party was popular with right-wingers in the pro-segregationist South. This was due to the historic role played by the Republican President *Abraham Lincoln* in the defeat of the Confederate States and the abolition of *slavery*.

denied powers: those powers that are formally forbidden to one or more branches of the federal government under the US *Constitution*.

- **e.g.** Article 1, section 9 of the Constitution states that 'No Title of Nobility shall be granted by the United States'.

differential turnout: the way in which recorded national figures for *turnout* in elections can disguise significant variation either by region or by socioeconomic group.

■ *e.g.* Turnout is higher amongst women than men. Old, white, wealthy voters are statistically more likely to turn out than young, poor voters from ethnic minorities. Turnout in key *swing states* or *districts* may also be higher than that in safe seats.

direct action: a form of *pressure group* action that most often favours the use of non-violent or violent physical protest over more traditional forms of protest such as letter writing, petitions and marches.

■ *e.g.* the intimidatory picketing of US *abortion* clinics by some *pro-life* groups.

■ *TIP* An increased willingness to engage in direct action is often seen as a sign that citizens are disillusioned with traditional forms of protest and/or dissatisfied with the work of their elected representatives.

■ *COMPARATIVE* In the UK, a rise in direct action pressure group activity has been accompanied by falling *turnout* in elections.

direct democracy: a pure form of democracy dating from *c.*500BC, where the 40,000 free men of Athens had the right to attend forum meetings at which certain policies could be approved or rejected.

● In the modern era the term has come to be associated with the greater use of devices such as *referendums, initiatives* and *recalls*; introduced to give citizens a more direct input into the business of government.

■ *TIP* Such devices are said to make governments more accountable, though it is argued that they also have the effect of undermining the principle of *representative democracy*. It is important to be able to contrast direct democracy with the style of representative democracy practised in many western liberal democracies.

■ *COMPARATIVE* Though the first referendum was not held within the UK until 1973 (in Northern Ireland), the government has made greater use of such devices in recent years (e.g. over devolution). However, there was only one UK-wide referendum between 1973 and 2007, namely the 1975 poll on whether or not the UK should remain in the EEC.

discharge petition: a motion requiring the *House Rules Committee* to give up a bill and return it for debate on the floor of the House.

● A discharge petition requires the support of an absolute majority of House Members (i.e. 218).

■ *e.g.* A discharge petition was needed to release the Shays-Meehan Campaign Finance Reform Bill (which later became the 2002 *BCRA*) from the House Rules Committee in 2001–02.

district: a population-based constituency within a state that returns a single member to the *House of Representatives*.

● The average population of a House district is around 650,000.

d

■ *e.g.* The less populous states (e.g. Alaska and Wyoming) consist of a single district. The most populous, California, had 53 House districts in the 2006 *mid-term elections*.

■ *TIP* The 435 House seats are re-apportioned between states as a result of the national census, which takes place every 10 years.

District of Columbia ('Washington DC'): the seat of the US federal government since 1800.

● Currently located on a plot of land that was originally ceded by the state of *Maryland*.

● The district itself was named in honour of Christopher Columbus, with the new capital taking its name from the first US president, *George Washington*.

● DC does not elect members to the US *House of Representatives* or to the *Senate* as it is not a state. It does, however, send a delegate to the House.

● Though the district now has some locally elected officials, its finances are still subject to congressional approval. The House of Representatives has a District of Columbia *standing committee*, which deals with measures relating to the government of the District.

■ *TIP* Since the *Twenty-Third Amendment* (1961) the district has held three votes in the *Electoral College*.

divided government: describes the situation where the presidency and one or both of the chambers of the US *Congress* are controlled by opposing parties.

■ *e.g.* Democrat successes in the 2006 *mid-term elections* meant that the Republican President *George W. Bush* had to face a Congress in which both the *House* and the *Senate* were Democrat controlled from the start of 2007.

■ *TIP* Divided government is often associated with gridlock. In fact, presidents facing a hostile *legislature* will often moderate their programmes and adopt bipartisan positions in order to improve their legislative success rate.

■ *COMPARATIVE* In the UK, there is a fusion of powers with the government being drawn from the majority party in the House of Commons. A party that does not control the Commons can be forced from government by a vote of confidence (e.g. James Callaghan's Labour administration in 1979).

DNC: see *Democratic National Committee*.

Dole, Bob (1923–): a former US Senator and failed Republican candidate in the 1996 presidential election, where he was defeated by incumbent President *Bill Clinton*.

● Part of Dole's time in the Senate was spent as Senate *majority leader*, a role in which he worked closely with Republican *Speaker* in the House, *Newt Gingrich*, in order to deliver on the promises made in the party's 1994 *Contract With America*.

Dole, Elizabeth (1936–): a Republican Senator and wife of failed 1996 Republican presidential candidate and one-time Senate *majority leader, Bob Dole*.

Dred Scott v Sandford (1857): a case in which the US *Supreme Court* ruled that a slave who sued for his freedom having been taken by his former owner to a free state (Illinois), should remain a slave.

- The judgement was handed down by Chief Justice Roger Taney who argued that black Americans could not be citizens of the United States.
- Taney's judgement also invalidated the Missouri Compromise, which had previously excluded *slavery* from the northern territories.

▨ *TIP* The implications of the ruling in this case and the inflammatory language used by Taney in his summing-up is seen as having contributed to the tension between 'slave states' and 'free states' that ultimately brought about the start of the *Civil War* in 1861.

dual federalism: the style of *federalism* in evidence between the 1780s and the 1920s. Dual federalism was based on the principle that the national and state governments had their own spheres of *authority* and that each was sovereign within its own sphere.

- This system operated fairly well as long as the federal government was small and was not interventionist. In the 1930s, however, things changed significantly as a result of the crisis that followed the *Wall Street Crash*.

Duckworth v Eagan (1989): a case in which the US *Supreme Court* ruled that the exact wording arrived at in the *Miranda* case did not have to be used for any subsequent confession to be valid. See *Miranda* v *Arizona*.

due process [of law]: the principle that citizens cannot be deprived of life, liberty or property without having the opportunity to demonstrate their innocence in a free and fair trial.

▨ *COMPARATIVE* The principle of due process of law is closely linked to the *rule of law*, a term commonly applied to both the UK and the USA.

▨ *TIP* Both the *Fifth* and *Fourteenth Amendments* to the US *Constitution* contain a due process clause.

Dukakis, Michael (1933–): former governor of Massachusetts and failed Democratic candidate in the 1988 presidential election.

- Dukakis was defeated by the incumbent *Vice-President George H. W. Bush* in 1988.
- The 1988 election is often remembered for the *Willie Horton attack-ad* that Bush used against Dukakis.

Edwards, John (1953–): a former US Senator and failed 2004 *Democratic Party* vice-presidential candidate; *running mate* to *John Kerry.*
- Edwards contested the race for the 2004 Democratic nomination with John Kerry, the man he ultimately joined on the party's *ticket.*
- In December 2006 he announced that he would be seeking his party's nomination in the 2008 presidential election.

***Edwards* v *Aquillard* (1987):** a case in which the US *Supreme Court* ruled that Louisiana's efforts to force the teaching of creationism alongside the study of evolution were in violation of the *First Amendment*'s Establishment Clause.

Ehrlichman, John (1925–99): a senior domestic policy advisor to US President *Richard Nixon.*
- Ehrlichman and *Bob Haldeman* (Nixon's *chief of staff*) were nicknamed 'the Berlin Wall' as a result of the extent to which they insulated the president from the outside world.
- Ehrlichman was deeply implicated in the *Watergate Scandal* and was ultimately sentenced to 18 months in prison.

Eighteenth Amendment (1819): established Prohibition in the USA.
- Banned the 'manufacture, sale, or transportation [including imports and exports] of intoxicating liquors'.
- **■ *TIP*** The Eighteenth Amendment was repealed by the *Twenty-First Amendment* in 1933.

Eighth Amendment (1791): best known for outlawing 'cruel and unusual punishment', though the amendment also banned excessive fines and the requirement of excessive bail payments.
- **■ *TIP*** The Eighth Amendment has long been associated with the application of the death penalty in the USA. See *capital punishment* and *Furman* v *Georgia.*
- **■ *COMPARATIVE*** In the UK such cruel and unusual punishment would be prohibited under the ban on torture included in Article 3 of the European Convention on Human Rights (ECHR), as incorporated into UK law under the 1998 Human Rights Act.

Eisenhower, Dwight D. (1890–1969): the thirty-fourth US *president,* 1953–61.

- Eisenhower had enjoyed a successful career in the military, most notably in the Second World War, before entering political life.
- His election in 1952 came at the height of the *Korean War.*

elastic clause: see *Necessary and Proper clause.*

elections: a process by which individuals are chosen to fill various public offices as a result of some form of popular vote.

Electoral College: the body that formally elects the US *president* following the public vote in November of an election year.

- The College consists of 538 votes (called Electoral College votes or ECVs). Each state casts a number of ECVs equal to its total representation in the US *Congress* (i.e. the number of House Members it has plus two votes in respect of its Senators).
- Although it is not a state, Washington DC currently holds three Electoral College votes — the number it would be entitled to if it were a state — as a result of the *Twenty-Third Amendment* to the US *Constitution* (1961).
- Most states give all of their ECVs to the candidate who wins the popular vote in the state. Nebraska and Maine, however, use the *Maine System.*
- A candidate becomes president by securing an overall majority of Electoral College votes (270). If no candidate reaches this mark the Electoral College is said to be 'hung'. A vote is then taken in the *House of Representatives* to decide who will become president. Each state has a single vote in this ballot. The *Senate* selects the *vice-president* in a similar vote.
- The individuals who cast votes in the Electoral College (Electors) are not the actual House Members or Senators from the state and they do not have to follow the wishes of their state's voters as expressed through the ballot box. See *rogue electors.*

■ *TIP* The College is said to be a relic of the *Founding Fathers'* fear of *mobocracy.*

■ *COMPARATIVE* Some have drawn parallels between the Electoral College in the USA and the way in which the UK prime minister gains his/her position by virtue of his/her party winning more than half of a series of *first-past-the-post* contests for Commons seats.

electoral system: a set of rules by which votes are translated into seats in a *legislature* or an individual is chosen to fill a named office.

- Electoral systems can be broadly divided into those that are majoritarian (e.g. *first-past-the-post*), those that are proportional (e.g. list systems) and those that are a combination of the two (hybrid systems such as AMS).

■ *e.g.* All major contests in the USA operate under the first-past-the-post (FPTP) system.

■ *COMPARATIVE* All UK elections were once conducted under FPTP. By 2007, however, the situation was more complicated with a range of systems in operation for different contests (e.g. FPTP, AMS, AV, STV).

electorate: a collective term for those individuals who are entitled to vote in a given *election*.

Eleventh Amendment (1798): prevented the US *Supreme Court* from hearing any case brought against an individual US state 'by citizens of another US state or by the citizens or subjects of any foreign state'.

elites theory: advanced by writers such as C. Wright Mills (in his book *The Power Elite*), the idea that a small elite controls *power* regardless of who may win *elections*.

- Elite theorists argue that senior figures in political life, the *media* and business are all part of the same elite who work with one another in order to advance their collective interests. See *iron triangle*.
- Elections are simply part of an illusion designed to keep those who are not part of the elite out of the loop.

■ *e.g.* From the perspective of elites theory, the presidential election of 2004 presented the voting public with a choice between two white, male, multi-millionaire Yale graduates who had both been members of the same secret society (*Skull and Bones*) whilst at university.

■ *TIP* It is helpful to be able to contrast elites theory with *pluralist theory*.

Emanuel, Rahm (1959–): chair of the Democratic Congressional Campaign Committee in 2006. Elected chair of the Democratic *caucus* in November 2006. Emanuel was credited with playing a part in the Democrats' success in the 2006 *mid-term elections*.

emergency powers: refers to the powers assigned to some political leaders and heads of state in the belief that, as *John Locke* noted, it is helpful 'in emergency [that] responsible leaders could resort to exceptional power'.

- In writing the US *Constitution* the *Founding Fathers* decided against explicitly assigning such emergency powers to the US *president*.
- As Congressman White of the First Congress noted, it would be better 'to extend his [the president's] power on some extraordinary occasion, even where he is not strictly justified by the Constitution, than the Legislature should grant him an improper power to be exercised at all times'.

■ *e.g.* The way in which both *Congress* and the US *Supreme Court* afforded President *George W. Bush* a degree of constitutional 'wiggle-room' in leading the US response to the attacks on *9/11* is often seen as evidence that formally codified emergency powers are not required.

■ *COMPARATIVE* In the UK, the prime minister has considerable room for manoeuvre in the event of an emergency through his exercise of prerogative powers.

EMILY's List: founded by Ellen Malcolm in 1985, a *political action committee* that aims to secure the election of more *pro-choice*, female *Democratic Party* candidates.

- The group provides such candidates with the kind of early contributions needed to get their campaigns off the ground. Once up-and-running with credible campaigns, such candidates are more able to raise their own campaign contributions.

▪ *TIP* The 'EMILY' in the group's name does not refer to an individual but is instead an acronym drawn from the opening line of the popular political saying 'early **m**oney **i**s **l**ike **y**east, because it helps to raise the dough'.

▪ *COMPARATIVE* The UK Labour Party has looked to achieve a similar increase in the number of female members in the Commons through the adoption of all-women shortlists in many safe Labour seats.

energising the base: see *building up the base*.

***Engel* v *Vitale* (1962):** a landmark case in which the US *Supreme Court* ruled (7:1) that states could not impose a set prayer on public schools because to do so would constitute a breach of the *First Amendment*'s Establishment Clause.

▪ *TIP* Justice Hugo Black took the view that the First Amendment should be taken literally, an approach referred to as First Amendment Absolutism. Writing the Court's opinion in the *Engel* case Black wrote that the use of public schools to encourage prayer was 'a practice wholly inconsistent with the Establishment Clause'.

▪ *COMPARATIVE* In the UK, there is an established church (the Anglican Church). As a result it has been common for state schools to be legally required to hold a daily act of collective worship.

Enron scandal: the scandal surrounding the collapse of the energy trading firm Enron and related allegations of flawed accountancy practices.

● The scandal had a political dimension. According to the *Guardian*, '188 House Members and 71 Senators had received campaign contributions from the company; five members of the Bush team had received cash from the company (some as directors or consultants); four had met with ENRON executives; and six had taken phonecalls from Enron in the run up to the collapse'.

entrenched: refers to a provision in any constitutional document that is protected from being changed quickly or easily by the existence of a formal and rigorous amendment process.

▪ *e.g.* The provisions of the US *Constitution* cannot be changed through the passage of a regular law through *Congress*. Such changes require a formal constitutional amendment that can only be secured with the support of sizeable supermajorities in Congress and amongst the various states.

▪ *COMPARATIVE* Entrenchment is difficult to achieve in the UK because in the absence of a codified and sovereign constitution, parliamentary statute is the highest source of UK law. In 2006, the Conservative leader David Cameron suggested that a form of entrenchment could be achieved by adding additional items to the list of measures that the Commons is not permitted to force through the Lords using the Parliament Act.

enumerated powers: those powers explicitly granted to particular institutions or assigned to federal or state governments under the US *Constitution*.

e

- *Congress*'s enumerated powers are set out in Article 1, section 8 of the Constitution, e.g. the power to coin money.

Environmental Protection Agency (EPA): established in 1970, an *executive agency* that possesses a broad remit for protecting public health and the natural environment. The head of the EPA is normally afforded *cabinet* rank.

EPA: see *Environmental Protection Agency.*

Equal Rights Amendment (ERA): an attempt to amend the US *Constitution* in such a way as to explicitly guarantee equal rights irrespective of gender.

- The proposed amendment secured the necessary two-thirds majorities in the *House* and the *Senate* in 1972 but was only ratified by 35 of the 38 states required, even though the deadline was put back to 1982.

ERA: see *Equal Rights Amendment.*

Escobedo v Illinois (1964): a case in which the US *Supreme Court* asserted that the accused had a constitutional right to legal counsel prior to trial.

ethnicity: the fact of belonging to a group that shares a common racial, cultural or national identity.

- Ethnicity is often said to be a key determinant of *voting behaviour.*

executive: the part of government that is charged with putting laws drawn up by the *legislature* into effect.

- The US *Constitution* vests sole executive power in the *president* and creates a formal separation between the executive, the legislature and the *judiciary.*

- **COMPARATIVE** In the UK, the legislature and the executive are fused with the latter being drawn from the former. The UK executive must retain the confidence of the Commons in order to remain in office. The US president is elected separately for a fixed term of 4 years and can only be removed through the *impeachment* process.

executive agency: a body created in order to address a particular area of policy with a greater degree of focus and independence of action than that afforded to an *executive department.*

- The heads of executive agencies — normally referred to as 'administrators' or 'directors' — are not ex officio members of the *cabinet* (i.e. members by right), though it has become common for some (e.g. the director of the Environmental Protection Agency) to be afforded cabinet rank.

- **e.g.** See *Environmental Protection Agency.*

- **COMPARATIVE** In the UK, such executive agencies, often referred to as Next Steps Agencies, proliferated in the 1980s and 1990s, e.g. the Child Support Agency.

executive agreement: a form of international agreement that is presented in such a way as to avoid the two-thirds *Senate* majority required for the *ratification* of *treaties.*

- The difficulty in securing the Senate supermajority needed to ratify a treaty (e.g. the rejection of the Treaty of Versailles) has led presidents to be more 'creative' in their dealings with foreign states.

- By the time of the *Nixon* presidency the number of treaties formally ratified each year was dwarfed by the number of executive agreements concluded.

- *e.g.* Between 1850 and 1900 there were 215 treaties and 238 executive agreements. In 1971 there were only 17 treaties compared to 214 executive agreements.

- *TIP* Congress tried to limit the use of executive agreements by passing the *Case Act (1972)*.

- *COMPARATIVE* The UK prime minister is not legally required to submit the treaties he signs to parliamentary approval as he concludes such agreements using the prerogative powers.

executive department: one of the oldest and most basic units of organisation in the US federal *executive*.

- There were originally three executive departments; those of State, War (which became Defense in 1949) and Treasury.

- The formal establishment of the Department of Homeland Security in 2003 brought the total number of executive departments to 15.

- Each department is headed by an appointed secretary who holds *cabinet* rank. US cabinet secretaries are normally specialists in their fields.

Executive Office of the President (EXOP): established in 1939 in response to a *Brownlow Committee* report of 1937, which had concluded that 'the President needs help'. EXOP consists of nearly 2,000 individuals.

- 40–50 senior staff have offices in the *West Wing* of the White House itself, the remainder are housed in adjacent accommodation such as the Eisenhower Executive Office building.

- *e.g.* EXOP includes bodies such as the *White House Staff (WHS)*, the *Office of Management and Budget (OMB)*, and the *National Security Council (NSC)*.

- *COMPARATIVE* Some argue that changes in the scale and structure of the Prime Minister's Office and the Cabinet Office in the UK have seen the emergence of something akin to EXOP — a UK West Wing.

executive privilege: theoretically based upon the sole executive power granted to the *president* under the US *Constitution*; the president's power to resist encroachments upon his *authority* within his area of constitutional competence.

- *e.g.* *Nixon* claimed that executive privilege gave him the right to resist demands that he release the *White House Tapes*. See *United States* v *Richard Nixon (1974)*.

- *TIP* The concept of executive privilege can be linked to the theory of the *unitary executive* advanced by *John Yoo* and others.

exit poll: a poll of voters taken immediately after they have exited polling stations.

- Exit polls are normally more reliable than regular *opinion polls* as they are taken after voters have cast their ballots.

- As they are only conducted once during the campaign, those companies commissioning exit polls often specify a far larger sample of voters than that used for a regular *polling* during the course of the campaign.

e

■ *TIP* The reliability of exit polls is dependent upon the extent to which those exiting polling stations are prepared to be honest about the way they have voted.

■ *e.g.* In the 2004 presidential election the CNN exit poll showed that *George W. Bush* had secured 11% of the black vote (up from 9% in 2000). Most commentators felt that the actual figure was probably nearer 14% but that a proportion of black voters were too embarrassed to admit that they had voted Republican.

■ *COMPARATIVE* The same thing happened in the UK in 1992 where the BBC exit poll showed a narrow lead for the Labour Party. It was said that some voters had been too embarrassed to admit that they had voted Conservative.

EXOP: see *Executive Office of the President.*

faithless elector: see *rogue elector*.

Falwell, Jerry (1933–2007): a US pastor and televangelist. Falwell founded the *Moral Majority* in 1979.

- Falwell's Moral Majority was one of a number of groups on the Christian right who supported the candidacies of Republican *Ronald Reagan* in the 1980s.

fat cats: those wealthy party contributors and local power-brokers who once controlled the governments of many US cities. See *machine politics*.

- The phrase 'fat cats' is often used in conjunction with another, *'smoke-filled rooms'*, as a way of suggesting the political sleaze or corruption in government.

FEC: see *Federal Election Commission*.

FECA: see *Federal Election Campaign Act, 1974*.

federal budget: a document setting out proposed funding for the coming fiscal year.

- The *president* submits his budget request to *Congress*.
- Congress arrives at a budget resolution based upon the president's request and individual appropriations bills, then allocates funding to specific federal government programmes.
- Congress does not always approve the president's budget request in its entirety.
- ▣ *e.g.* Both *Ronald Reagan* and *Bill Clinton* had budgets rejected during their time in office.
- ▣ *COMPARATIVE* A UK government that failed to secure the legislature's approval for its budget would almost certainly face a vote of confidence.

federal bureaucracy: the unelected part of the US government that is responsible for putting policy into effect. The terms federal bureaucracy and federal *civil service* are often used as synonyms for one another.

- Includes the organisation and staff of the various *executive departments*, *executive agencies* and regulatory commissions.
- ▣ *TIP* The US *cabinet* is technically part of the federal bureaucracy as it consists of unelected bureaucrats rather than elected politicians.

federal courts: those courts that form part of the federal judicial system as opposed to those operating under the jurisdiction of an individual state.

- Includes the US *Supreme Court*, 13 federal Courts of Appeal (11 Circuit Courts of Appeal, one in Washington DC and one Court of Appeal for the federal circuit), 94 District Courts, and a number of smaller specialised courts such as the US Claims Court and the US Court of International Trade.
- **e.g.** A case involving a federal statute would normally be held in a US District Court. Any appeal from the case would normally be heard in one of the federal Courts of Appeal.
- **TIP** It is worth remembering that 95% of court cases are not heard in federal courts but in state trial courts.

Federal Election Campaign Act (FECA) (1974): building on an Act first passed in 1971, FECA (1974) established the *Federal Election Commission* and placed limits on campaign contributions.

- The Act imposed a $1,000 limit on individual contributions to a campaign. This was later increased to $2,000 under the *Bipartisan Campaign Finance Reform Act (BCRA 2002)*.
- *Political action committees* (PACs) were allowed to donate up to $5,000 per candidate, per election cycle.
- Matching funds (state funding) were available for those candidates who could demonstrate widespread support and agreed to be bound by an overall spending limit.
- Some of the Act's provisions were struck down in the *Supreme Court* case *Buckley* v *Valeo (1976)*.
- **TIP** The kind of campaign contributions limited by FECA (1974) are generally referred to as '*hard money*' contributions. A subsequent Campaign Finance Act in 1979 opened up what became known as the '*soft money* loophole'. Money given to help fund measures aimed at increasing *voter registration* and *turnout* was exempted from the 1974 Act.

Federal Election Commission (FEC): an independent regulatory agency that was established under the *Federal Election Campaign Act of 1974* to oversee and enforce federal election regulations.

federalism: a system of government involving a central *authority* with its own institutions and a number of regional authorities that exercise autonomous political *power* within their areas of responsibility.

- The *Founding Fathers* adopted a federal structure for the government created under the US *Constitution* devised at the *Philadelphia Constitutional Convention* of 1787. Once adopted it replaced the looser confederal system that had existed under the *Articles of Confederation* between 1781 and 1788.
- **e.g.** State governments have control over issues ranging from the existence and application of the *death penalty* to the age at which individuals can lawfully marry. The federal government controls areas ranging from defence to coinage.
- **TIP** Federalism is not as fixed as it might at first appear. The relationship between individual states and the federal government has gone through a

number of phases since the Constitution was ratified. See *dual federalism, cooperative federalism,* and *new federalism.*

■ *COMPARATIVE* Devolution in the UK is not analogous to US federalism as the Westminster Parliament retains the power to limit or remove the autonomy of devolved institutions as has happened in respect of Northern Ireland between 2002 and 2007.

Federal Trade Commission: an *Independent Regulatory Commission* established in 1914 by the Federal Trade Commission Act.

● The Commission is charged with the tasks of preventing unfair competition, the operation of cartels, and misleading advertising.

Fifteenth Amendment (1870): prevented the federal government or individual state governments from denying citizens the right to vote on the grounds of race, colour or 'previous condition of servitude'.

Fifth Amendment (1791): guaranteed *due process of law* and thereby protected US citizens from arbitrary imprisonment.

● The Fifth Amendment also included the double jeopardy clause, protecting citizens for being tried repeatedly for the same crime.

● A further clause guaranteed the accused's right to silence.

■ *COMPARATIVE* In the UK, the right to silence and the notion of double jeopardy were both brought into question as a result of changes introduced by New Labour between 1997 and 2007.

filibuster: talking at length in the *Senate*, either individually or as part of a group, in order to extend debate to a point where a bill is 'talked out of time' without there being any opportunity for a formal vote to be taken.

● The freedom to talk at length during debates is considered a Senate privilege. In contrast, the length of time that a member of the *House of Representatives* can speak in floor debates has been strictly limited in the modern era.

● There are no rules governing what Senators may or may not talk about when leading a filibuster. Some have gone as far as reading pages from telephone directories or reciting family recipes.

■ *e.g.* Senator *Strom Thurmond* of South Carolina spoke for 24 hours and 18 minutes against the 1957 Civil Rights Act. A group of southern Democrats conducted an 83-day group filibuster against the *1964 Civil Rights Act.*

■ *TIP* A filibuster can be ended by the means of a *cloture motion.* This device brings the debate to an end and results in an immediate vote being taken on the measure in question.

■ *COMPARATIVE* In the UK, Private Members' Bills (PMBs) are particularly vulnerable to filibustering. This is partly because the time available for the discussion of non-government legislation is so strictly limited, and also because the controversial nature of many PMBs is more likely to provoke such spoiling tactics.

Fillmore, Millard (1800–74): the thirteenth US *president*, 1850–53.

- The last president to be elected who was not a Democrat or a Republican; Fillmore was a Whig.

First Amendment (1791): the first of the ten amendments that comprise the *Bill of Rights*, this provides a range of guarantees relating to the *freedom of speech*, the freedom of religion and the freedom of protest.

- The first two clauses of the Amendment, the Establishment Clause and the Free Exercise Clause, are concerned with the separation between church and state.
- The Amendment also protects the freedom of speech and of the press, the right of assembly, and the right to petition for redress of grievances.

■ *TIP* The full extent of the rights protected under the First Amendment cannot really be understood without reference to subsequent US *Supreme Court* cases, e.g. *Engel* v *Vitale (1962)* and *Hustler Magazine* v *Falwell (1988)*.

first-past-the-post: an electoral system under which the winning candidate need only secure one vote more than his or her nearest rival.

- This is the system employed in some form or another in most US elections at state and federal level.
- It is simple to operate but has a tendency to result in large numbers of wasted votes.

■ *e.g.* In 1992 *Ross Perot* secured 19% of the popular vote yet failed to secure any of the 538 *Electoral College* votes. This outcome resulted from the fact that 48 of the 50 US states awarded all of their Electoral College votes on a first-past-the-post basis.

527 groups: named after the section of the US tax-code that made them tax-exempt, these groups have campaigned for or against candidates at election time.

- 527s proliferated because they worked within the regulations brought in by the *Bipartisan Campaign Reform Act (BCRA, 2002)* and the earlier *Federal Election Campaign Act (FECA, 1974)*.
- 527s were relatively free to conduct issue-based campaigns, so long as they did not accept money from trade unions or corporations, and remained independent of party campaign managers or candidates.

■ *e.g.* The Swift Boat Veterans for Truth did the *Kerry* campaign serious damage in 2004 by attacking his military record in Vietnam.

flag desecration: often undertaken as part of a political protest, any act which involves an attempt to wilfully deface or destroy a flag.

- In the 1990s there were several unsuccessful attempts to amend the US *Constitution* in such a way as to outlaw flag desecration (see below).

■ *TIP* The *Supreme Court* has ruled that flag-burning is a form of expressive conduct protected under the *First Amendment*. See *Texas* v *Johnson (1989)*.

Flag Desecration Amendment: a proposed amendment to the US *Constitution* that would outlaw the desecration of the American flag (see above).

- Many saw amending the Constitution as a means of preventing the *Supreme Court* from ruling that flag-burning was a form of protected speech as it had done in *Texas* v *Johnson (1989)*.

- *e.g.* In 2005 a Flag Desecration Amendment passed the *House of Representatives* with the required two-thirds majority needed for an amendment to the US Constitution. In 2006 a similar vote in the US Senate failed to achieve the two-thirds mark by a single vote.

Florida: the twenty-seventh state; joined the *Union* in 1845.

- Florida was the key '*swing state*' in the disputed 2000 presidential election. See *Bush* v *Gore (2000)*.

focus group: a small, representative sample of between 10 and 20 individuals who are asked to express and discuss their views on a range of issues determined by those who have assembled the group.

- Focus groups are often used by political parties or a candidate's campaign team as a means of dry testing policies or identifying weaknesses in their opponents' or their own campaigns.

FOIA: see *Freedom of Information Act (1966)*.

Foley, Tom (1929–): former Democrat member and one-time *Speaker of the House of Representatives*. First elected in 1964, Foley left the House in 1995.

Forbes, Steve (1947–): a candidate for the Republican nomination in the 1996 and 2000 presidential elections. Later acted as an advisor to 2008 Republican presidential hopeful Rudolph Giuliani.

Ford, Gerald R. (1913–2006): the thirty-eighth US *president*, 1974–77.

- Ford was never elected as either *vice-president* or *president*. He was chosen as vice-president in 1973 following the resignation of incumbent *Spiro Agnew*. Ford then assumed the role of president following the resignation of *Richard Nixon* the following year.

- One of Ford's earliest and also most controversial acts was to issue a pardon that spared his predecessor from any criminal prosecution that might have arisen out of the *Watergate Scandal*.

- Though Ford initially stated that he would not seek the Republican nomination in the 1976 presidential election, he did run but lost to the *Democratic Party* candidate *Jimmy Carter*.

- *TIP* The reaction to the manner of Nixon's fall from grace saw the emergence of a far more assertive *Congress*. As a result, Ford struggled to impose his domestic agenda.

Founding Fathers: the 55 delegates who met at the *Philadelphia Convention* in 1787 and agreed a new *constitution* to replace the *Articles of Confederation* that had been in place since 1781.

- All of the former British colonies were represented at the Convention apart from Rhode Island.
- Several leading Founding Fathers went on to serve as *president* in the newly formed *Union*.
- ▨ *e.g.* *George Washington*, who had presided over the Philadelphia Convention, served as president between 1789 and 1797. *Thomas Jefferson*, who had played a large part in drafting the *Declaration of Independence*, was president between 1801 and 1809.

Fourteenth Amendment (1865): notable for enshrining the principle that no person should be deprived of 'life, liberty, or property, without *due process of law*'.
- The Amendment also guaranteed 'equal protection under the law'.
- ▨ *TIP* This guarantee of equal protection under the law has been at the heart of a number of crucial *Supreme Court* judgements, e.g. see *Brown* v *Board of Education (1954)* and *Bush* v *Gore (2000)*.
- ▨ *COMPARATIVE* In the UK, the Rule of Law, as defined by A. V. Dicey in 1885, enshrines the principle of equal protection under the law.

Fourth Amendment (1791): concerned with protecting citizens and their property from unreasonable searches and seizures.
- It states that search warrants can only be issued where there is 'probable cause'.
- ▨ *TIP* The Fourth Amendment provides part of the constitutional justification for the 'zone of privacy' identified by the US *Supreme Court* in cases such as *Griswold* v *Connecticut (1965)*.

franchise: the right to vote.
- In the United States the right to vote has been extended both by the means of constitutional amendment and through the passing of regular laws.
- ▨ *e.g.* The *Voting Rights Act (1970)* gave all those over the age of 18 the right to vote in federal elections and the *Twenty-Sixth Amendment* (1971) extended this entitlement to all US elections.
- ▨ *TIP* Though the *Fifteenth Amendment* (1870) legally barred states from denying citizens the right to vote on the basis of colour or race, many states circumvented this prohibition by using more indirect ways of limiting the franchise. See *Grandfather Clause*.

Franklin, Benjamin (1706–90): a well known philosopher, author and politician. He is one of the better known *Founding Fathers* and a key figure in securing the alliance with the French that made independence possible.

Franklin D. Roosevelt (1882–1945): the thirty-second *president* of the USA. He served from 1933 until his death in 1945.
- Victorious in four consecutive presidential elections (1932, 1936, 1940 and 1944) in an era before the *Twenty-Second Amendment* (1951) limited the president to two 4-year terms.

- He was closely associated with his *New Deal* programme, which sought to address the problems caused by the *Great Depression*.

Freedom of Information Act (FOIA) (1966): signed into law by President *Lyndon Johnson* in 1966, this Act allows, upon request, for the release of material held by the US government that is not currently in the public domain.

- The Act exempts certain sensitive documents from being disclosed.

▓ *TIP* The Freedom of Information Act is a good example of how some of the rights available to US citizens are given to them by regular laws, as opposed to being explicitly set out in the US *Constitution*.

▓ *COMPARATIVE* Often compared with the UK's Freedom of Information Act of 2000, which came into force in January 2005, the mandatory disclosure procedures imposed by the US Act give those requesting information significantly more leverage than is the case under the UK Act.

freedom of speech: in its broadest sense, the belief that the state should not be able to regulate either the spoken or the printed word.

- The US *Supreme Court* has recognised two broad categories of speech, that which is 'protected' and that which is 'unprotected'.

- Protected speech may consist of pure speech (spoken or written) or what is known as expressive conduct, i.e. an action that is designed to convey a particular message, e.g. *flag desecration*. Of the two forms of protected speech, the Supreme Court gives greater protection to the former.

- Unprotected speech can itself be sub-divided into three further categories: libel, obscenity, and fighting words (words that according to the Court are 'designed to harm emotionally or to trigger a hostile reaction').

▓ *e.g.* The Court has ruled that although semi-nude erotic dancing is protected under the *First Amendment* as a form of expressive conduct, a state may impose limits upon totally nude erotic dancing.

front-loading: a process whereby increasingly large numbers of states move their *primary elections* or *caucuses* ever-earlier in the presidential election year.

- States front-load their primaries in the belief that earlier contests have a greater influence over the eventual outcome of the nomination process than those later in the season.

- In 1980, just 11 states held their primaries before the end of March. By 2004 the figure was 36.

▓ *e.g.* In 2007 California governor *Arnold Schwarzenegger* signed legislation that moved the state's 2008 primary to 5 February, making it one of the earliest contests in the primary season.

▓ *TIP* One consequence of front-loading is that the nomination race is often over as a contest by the start of March. It is therefore even more crucial for candidates to get off to a good start and gain quick momentum (the 'Big Mo') by winning early victories in states such as New Hampshire and Iowa.

frost-belt: a region of the USA generally taken as including the Great Lakes, parts of the upper Midwest and the northeastern states.

- Census returns in the latter part of the twentieth century appeared to show a shift in population from the frost-belt to the *sun-belt.*

Fukuyama, Francis (1952–): a philosopher, political economist and author.

- He is best known for his book, *The End of History and the Last Man*, in which he prophesises the eventual triumph of political and economic liberalism.

***Furman* v *Georgia* (1972):** a landmark case in which the US *Supreme Court* ruled that the way in which the state of Georgia had applied the death penalty constituted a form of 'cruel and unusual punishment' that violated the *Eighth Amendment* to the US Constitution.

- *Furman* v *Georgia* was one of a number of cases that resulted in *capital punishment* effectively being stopped in the USA between 1973 and 1976.
- See also *Atkins* v *Virginia (2002)* and *Roper* v *Simmons (2005).*

Garfield, James A. (1831–81]: the twentieth US *president* who served for a little over 6 months between March and September, 1881.

- The second US president to be assassinated; *Abraham Lincoln* being the first.

gender gap: the gap between the support given to certain candidates by women and the support given to the same range of candidates by men.

- In the USA female voters have traditionally been more likely to vote Democrat than Republican whereas the reverse is true of male voters.

■ *e.g.* In the 2004 presidential election, which *George W. Bush* won by a clear margin, women favoured the Democrat *John Kerry* (51% Kerry, 48% Bush) whilst men favoured Bush (55% Bush 44% Kerry).

■ *TIP* Some argue that the high levels of female support for *Democratic Party* candidates can be attributed to the party's *pro-choice* stance on the issue of *abortion* and its support for *gun control.*

■ *COMPARATIVE* In the UK, the gender gap traditionally saw greater support for the Conservative Party amongst women. Since 1997, however, this gap has closed, a result perhaps of the way in which New Labour sought to engage with female voters, e.g. through the adoption of all-women shortlists and through its policies.

George W. Bush v Al Gore (2000): see *Bush* v *Gore (2000).*

Georgia: the fourth state; joined the *Union* in 1788.

Gephardt, Dick (1941–): a Democratic member of the *House of Representatives* between 1977 and 2005 where he served as *majority leader* (1989–95) and *minority leader* (1995–2003). He was a failed candidate for the Democratic presidential nomination in 1988 and 2004.

gerrymandering: the practice of manipulating the boundaries between electoral *districts* in such as way as to maximise one's own chances of success.

- The *Supreme Court* has ruled that such practices are inconsistent with the *Fourteenth Amendment* because they deny voters in the districts concerned 'equal protection under the law'.

■ *e.g.* The term has its origins in the way in which in 1812 Massachusetts Governor Elbridge Gerry redrew his state's congressional districts in order to benefit his party. The 'mandering' part of the term resulted from the fact that one of the districts created was said to resemble a salamander.

get out the vote campaigns (GOTV): referring to any effort to increase the number of registered voters who turn out on election day.

● GOTV campaigns often follow on in the wake of *voter registration drives*.

▥ *TIP* Contributions towards GOTV campaigns and voter registration drives were classified as unregulated '*soft money*' under the 1979 changes to the *Federal Election Campaign Act (1974)*.

Gettysburg Address: one of the most famous speeches in US history, delivered by *Abraham Lincoln* at the dedication of the Soldiers' National Cemetery at Gettysburg, Pennsylvania in 1863.

● The address came 4½ months after the *Union* armies had defeated Confederate forces at the Battle of Gettysburg.

▥ *e.g.* Lincoln's speech asserted his belief that the survival of 'government of the people, by the people, and for the people' would ensure that those who had fallen in battle had not died in vain.

▥ *TIP* The Battle of Gettysburg was a decisive turning point in the American *Civil War* (1861–65).

***Gideon* v *Wainwright* (1963):** a case in which the US *Supreme Court* ruled that legal counsel had to be provided to the poor free of charge.

● The Court ruled that such free counsel was required under the 'due process' clause of the *Fourteenth Amendment* and the *Sixth Amendment* provision that all of those accused in criminal prosecutions should have 'the Assistance of Counsel' for their defence.

Gingrich, Newt (1943–): a Republican member of the *House of Representatives* who served as *Speaker* between 1995 and 1999.

● Closely associated with the Republican takeover of the House and the *Senate* following their successes in the 1994 *mid-term elections*, Gingrich was co-author of the party's *platform* in those elections, known as the '*Contract with America*'.

Ginsburg, Douglas Howard (1946–): a Harvard law professor and chief judge of the US Court of Appeals for the District of Columbia Circuit from 1986 (see *federal courts*). He was nominated as associate justice for the US *Supreme Court* in 1987.

● Ginsburg was chosen to replace Lewis Powell on the Supreme Court after *Ronald Reagan*'s first nominee, *Robert Bork*, had been rejected by the US *Senate*.

● The vacancy was eventually filled by *Anthony Kennedy* after Ginsburg withdrew his nomination.

Ginsburg, Ruth Bader (1933–): a US *Supreme Court* justice nominated by President *Bill Clinton* in 1993. She was formerly a federal judge on the US Court of Appeals for the District of Columbia Circuit and a university academic.

● She was considered one of the more liberal members of the *Rehnquist* and *Roberts* Courts.

● The second woman to serve on the Court, the first being *Sandra Day O'Connor*.

g

Goldwater, Barry (1909–98): a five-term Republican member of the US *Senate* representing Arizona; Goldwater was his party's candidate in the 1964 presidential election.

- The Democrat's 1964 campaign ads characterised Goldwater as a right-wing reactionary in both domestic and foreign policy.
- He was heavily defeated by the incumbent Democratic President *Lyndon Johnson.*

GOP: see *Grand Old Party.*

Gore, Al (1948–): former Democrat member of the *House of Representatives* and later the US *Senate* who served as *vice-president* between 1993 and 2001. Defeated *Democratic Party* candidate in the 2000 presidential election. Since his defeat, he has emerged as a campaigner on environmental issues.

- During his time as vice-president Gore was credited with a number of successes including the signing of the *North American Free Trade Agreement (NAFTA).*
- Gore lost the 2000 presidential election despite having won around 540,000 votes more nationally than his Republican opponent *George W. Bush.*

Grandfather Clause: originally part of the Jim Crow Laws that were used to prevent black Americans from voting in the *Deep South* between 1890 and the mid-1920s. The clause granted the right to vote to those who had held the franchise before the *Civil War,* and their descendants.

Grand Old Party (GOP): the traditional nickname for the *Republican Party.*

Grant, Ulysses S. (1822–85): the eighteenth US *president,* 1869–77.

- Grant is widely regarded as the *Union's* leading general in the American *Civil War.*

Gratz v Bollinger (2003): a case in which the US *Supreme Court* ruled against the *affirmative action*-based undergraduate admissions programme employed by the University of Michigan.

- The Court held that the way in which the programme automatically gave black, Hispanic, or American-Indian applicants a 'head-start' of 20 of the 150 points needed for admission was overly mechanistic. See also *Grutter v Bollinger (2003).*

Great Depression: a global economic down-turn prompted by the collapse of the US stock market on 29 October 1929. This collapse is commonly referred to as the *Wall Street Crash* or 'Black Tuesday'.

Great Society: a label applied to the domestic policy agenda of US President *Lyndon Johnson,* from 1963 to 1969.

- Johnson's programme included a range of measures that aimed to tackle issues of racial inequality, poverty, and urban regeneration.
- Some have compared the Great Society programme to *Franklin D. Roosevelt's New Deal* programme of the 1930s.

■ *TIP* Johnson's Great Society could be seen as a continuation, in part at least, of *John F. Kennedy's New Frontier* programme, which had been cut short by the president's assassination.

g

Green Party: a permanent US *third party* (i.e. minor party), active since the 1980s and best known for the candidacy of *Ralph Nader* in the 2000 presidential election.

▨ *COMPARATIVE* The UK Green Party has had more success in elections to the European Parliament (securing two seats in 1999 and in 2004) than it has in general election, where it is yet to win a seat. The party's success in European elections may reflect the use of the regional party list electoral system or the fact that its policies are seen as being more relevant at a supranational level.

gridlock: describes the situation in which the US *executive* is at loggerheads with one or both chambers of the *legislature*.

- Gridlock in the US system is often associated with the presence of *divided government*.

▨ *e.g.* In 1995 the Democrat President *Bill Clinton*'s *budget* was blocked by the Republican-controlled *Congress*.

▨ *COMPARATIVE* Gridlock is rare in the UK because the party in government normally holds a working majority in the House of Commons.

Griswold v Connecticut (1965): a case in which the US *Supreme Court* struck down a Connecticut law that banned the use of contraception.

- The Court's ruling was based on a constitutional 'zone of privacy' that it argued was implied by the *First, Fourth, Fifth* and *Ninth Amendments*.

- The Court argued that it had the *authority* to apply this general ruling to individual states such as Connecticut under the *due process* clause of the *Fourteenth Amendment*.

▨ *TIP* This case was significant because it went some way towards providing the legal basis for the landmark *Roe* v *Wade* case in 1973.

Grutter v Bollinger (2003): a case in which the US *Supreme Court* ruled that the University of Michigan Law School's *affirmative action*-based admissions programme was permissible under the US *Constitution* because it took an individualised approach to assessing the racial profile of its applicants rather than simply applying the kind of across-the-board adjustment that had been struck down in *Gratz* v *Bollinger (2003)*.

Guantanamo Bay: generally refers to the US detainment camp and military prison sited at Guantanamo Bay, Cuba.

- From 2002 the camp was used to hold those suspected of having links with al-Qaeda or the Taliban. Many of these prisoners were captured in Afghanistan or Pakistan before being transported to Guantanamo.

▨ *e.g.* A number of British citizens were amongst those originally held at Guantanamo Bay. They included Birmingham-born Moazzam Begg, who was returned to the UK without charge in January 2005.

▨ *TIP* The US government's use of the camp was widely seen as a means of denying inmates the kinds of rights that they would be entitled to if they were held on the US mainland.

g

■ *COMPARATIVE* In the UK, the Anti-terrorism, Crime and Security Act (2001) led to the indefinite detention of terrorist suspects without trial. The Lords' ruling that this punishment was incompatible with the European Convention on Human Rights prompted the introduction of the Prevention of Terrorism Act (2005). This Act replaced indefinite detention with control orders.

Gulf of Tonkin Resolution: a resolution that gave President *Lyndon Johnson* the power to use all necessary force to defend American interests in southeast Asia. It was passed in 1964 in response to an attack on US naval forces in the Gulf of Tonkin.

● The resolution's importance lies in the fact that it provided the legal authority for the escalation of US involvement in Vietnam, without the need for a formal declaration of war by *Congress.*

gun control: any effort to limit the free availability of firearms. See *Second Amendment* and *Brady Bill.*

Haldeman, H. R. ('Bob') (1926–93): White House *chief of staff* under *Nixon*.
- Implicated in criminal activities connected to the *Watergate Scandal*, he was later sentenced to 18 months in prison.
- A close associate of *John Ehrlichman*, another of Nixon's *aides*.
- Haldeman was accused of allowing the president to become dangerously insulated from what was being done in his name.
- *e.g.* It was said that Haldeman saw the president seven times more than any other official. All phone calls, information and requests for meetings with the president had to pass through him. As Haldeman explained: 'Rather than the president telling someone to do something, I'll tell the guy. If he wants to find out something from somebody, I'll do it.'

Hamilton, Alexander (1755–1804): a leading *Founding Father* at the 1787 *Philadelphia Constitutional Convention*, Hamilton co-authored the Federalist Papers.

Harding, Warren G. (1865–1923): the twenty-ninth US *president*, 1921–23.

hard money: campaign contributions that are regulated under the *Federal Election Campaign Act (1974)*, as amended by subsequent Acts.
- The Act allowed individual contributions of $1,000 per candidate, per election. It also allowed each *political action committee* (PAC) to contribute up to $5,000 per candidate. The hard money limit for individual contributions was raised to $2,000 under the *Bipartisan Campaign Finance Reform Act (BCRA)* of 2002.

Harrison, Benjamin (1833–1901): the twenty-third US *president*, 1889–93.

Harris v McRae (1980): a case in which the US *Supreme Court* upheld the constitutionality of the *Hyde Amendment*.

Harris v New York (1971): a case in which the US *Supreme Court* ruled that confessions taken in violation of the Miranda ruling could still be used for limited purposes. See *Miranda v Arizona (1966)*.

Harrison, William H. (1773–1841): the ninth US president. Harrison died a month after his inauguration in 1841; the shortest tenure of any president.

Hawaii: the fiftieth state; joined the *Union* in 1959.

Hayes, Rutherford B. (1822–93): the nineteenth US president, 1877–81.

Haynesworth, Clement (1912–89): nominated to the US *Supreme Court* by *Richard Nixon* in 1969, Haynesworth's appointment was later rejected by the US *Senate*, 55:45, amidst concerns over his earlier support for segregation, and alleged judicial impropriety.

healthcare reform (re: Bill Clinton)**:** the main plank in *Bill Clinton*'s 1992 presidential election *platform.*

- After his inauguration, Bill Clinton appointed his wife, *Hillary Clinton*, to head the Task Force on National Health Care Reform.

- Despite Democratic control of the *House* and the *Senate*, the universal health-care scheme proposed under the plan was rejected by *Congress* in 1994.

- Many regarded this failure as a result of *lobbying* undertaken by companies providing private health insurance (HMOs), those in the medical profession, and other interested parties.

- *e.g.* The most famous public attack on the plan came in the form of the 'Harry and Louise' ad, a short *attack-ad* where the two characters were seen discussing the plan's perceived complexity and bureaucratic nature.

- *TIP* The failure of the plan is often falsely used as an example of how Clinton struggled with *divided government* following Republican successes in the 1994 *mid-term elections*. In fact, the plan was rejected by a Democrat-controlled Congress.

hegemonic theory (re: the media)**:** that the outlook of journalists in both the print and broadcast *media* is shaped by their own socioeconomic background. Consequently, they write from a particular perspective, however unconscious their bias might be.

Helms, Jesse (1921–): a former member of the US *Senate* representing North Carolina. Also one-time chair of the Senate Foreign Relations Committee.

- Helms was regarded as a traditional *Deep South* conservative. He was a leading figure on the Christian right.

Hispanics: referring to those citizens descended entirely or in part from natives of Spanish-speaking Central America, South America, or from Spain itself.

- A term recognised by the US government in the 1970s and used in the Census for the first time in 1980.

- *TIP* As a 'group' US Hispanics are neither homogenous nor particularly cohesive. There is no obvious reason, for example, why Cuban exiles should be categorised alongside Mexican-Americans. It is also worth remembering that Hispanics are divided between those categorised under the Census as 'white Hispanics' and those who are 'black'.

Homeland Security Department (DHS): originally the Office of Homeland Security, created by President *George W. Bush* in the wake of the attacks on *9/11*. It became the fifteenth *executive department* in 2003.

- The DHS is charged with the task of anticipating — ideally preventing — domestic emergencies, as well as coordinating the response to such emergencies.

- Most DHS work since 2003 has been concerned with protecting the US against terrorist threats against domestic targets.
- Since 2003 the DHS has become one of the largest executive departments, employing close to 200,000 staff.
- **TIP** The DHS works closely with the Homeland Security Council created in 2001. This council originally consisted of the *president* and the *vice-president*, the head of the Office of Homeland Security, the heads of a number of executive departments (e.g. Defense, Treasury, and Transportation) plus key security officials such as the directors of the FBI and the CIA.

honeymoon period: the weeks immediately following a president's inauguration where *Congress*, the *media*, and the broader American public are more willing to give the chief executive the benefit of the doubt.

Hoover, Herbert (1874–1964): the thirty-first US *president*, 1929–33.

- Hoover's single term in office is often remembered for the *Great Depression* that hit the USA in the wake of the *Wall Street Crash* of 29 October 1929.
- His failure to bring about a revival of the US economy paved the way for the election of *Franklin D. Roosevelt* in 1932.

Hoovervilles: literally 'Hoover-towns', the name given to the ramshackle temporary houses, tents and other forms of shelter that proliferated amid the unemployment and homelessness caused by the *Great Depression*.

- The term was meant as a criticism of President *Herbert Hoover*'s failure to deal with the consequences of the *Wall Street Crash*.

Horton, Willie (1951–): convicted murderer who when released from prison while serving a life sentence committed a rape and armed robbery against a woman. See *attack-ads*.

House of Representatives: the larger of the two chambers in the US *legislature*.

- It has 435 members, apportioned between states in broad proportion to population.
- Each House Member represents a single *district* within a state.
- Elections for all of the seats in the House are held every 2 years.
- **e.g.** In 2006 the Democrats won 232 seats to the Republicans' 203.
- **TIP** House Members are often referred to simply as *Congressmen*. As the US Congress consists of the House and the *Senate*, however, it is probably clearer to refer to members of this larger chamber as House Members.

House Rules Committee: see *Rules Committee*.

Humphrey, Hubert (1911–78): a Democratic member of the *Senate* (1949–65) and majority *whip* (1961–65), Humphrey later served as *vice-president* to *Lyndon Johnson* (1965–69). He won the Democratic nomination in the presidential election of 1968, losing narrowly to the Republican candidate, *Richard Nixon*. He later returned to the US Senate (1971–78).

- Humphrey won his party's nomination for the 1968 presidential election despite the fact that he had secured less than 2% of the vote in the *primaries*. This was possible because he was popular with those National Convention delegates who had been chosen by the state party bosses.

■ *TIP* The fallout from the 1968 nomination process resulted in major changes in *Democratic Party* rules ahead of the 1972 presidential election. See *McGovern-Fraser Commission*.

hundred days: originally refers to the period of intense activity at the start of *Franklin D. Roosevelt*'s first term in office. More recently, it is used to refer to a period of time after which it is acceptable for a new president to be judged on his achievements.

● During his hundred days Roosevelt launched numerous *initiatives* in the hope of bringing the USA out of the *Great Depression*. Some policies had been held over from *Herbert Hoover*'s term in office, others were Roosevelt's own ideas, or the pet projects of *Congressmen*.

Hustler Magazine v Falwell (1988): a case in which the US *Supreme Court* ruled that the evangelist *Jerry Falwell* was not entitled to compensation for the emotional distress caused by a spoof story run in the adult-only magazine.

● The magazine piece had parodied Falwell as a drunk who had engaged in an incestuous sexual liaison with his mother.

● The District Court had ruled that while no one would take the story as the kind of 'factual assertion' that might constitute libel of a public figure, Falwell was entitled to damages of $200,000 for 'intentional infliction of emotional distress'.

● The Supreme Court over-ruled this award of damages, arguing that there was a history of satirical caricature in the USA, which was clearly protected by the *First Amendment*.

● The story surrounding the case was later made into the film, *The People v Larry Flint*.

■ *TIP* Libel is one of the three forms of unprotected speech, the others being obscenity and fighting words. See *First Amendment*.

Hyde Amendment: an amendment applied to appropriations bills that has the effect of preventing federal monies being used to fund *abortions*.

● The original amendment was introduced in 1976 by Henry Hyde, then a Republican House Member on the Christian right.

● Since then a number of variations on the original amendment have been in force.

● The amendment was part of a broader effort to bring about a de facto end to abortion (by removing funding) as opposed to attempting to ban the practice itself (de jure). The US *Supreme Court* has been far more willing to accept such de facto limitations than it has been to overturn the broad principles established in *Roe v Wade (1973)*.

■ *e.g.* The US Supreme Court upheld the constitutionality of the Hyde Amendment in *Harris v McRae (1980)*.

Idaho: the forty-third state; joined the *Union* in 1890.

ideology: a term dating from the eighteenth century, referring to a coherent set of ideas or ideals that shapes one's actions and outlook.

Illinois: the twentieth state; joined the *Union* in 1818.

impeachment: often used in reference to the US *president*, the formal process under which an individual may be charged and ultimately removed from office for crimes against the state.

- In the USA, impeachment is a two-stage process. First the *House of Representatives* must pass articles of impeachment by a simple majority. Second, the accused is tried in the US *Senate* where a two-thirds majority will result in him/her being convicted and removed from office.

- **e.g.** Presidents *Andrew Johnson* and *Bill Clinton* were impeached though neither was convicted in the Senate. Johnson survived the Senate vote by a single vote.

- **TIP** A defendant is said to have been impeached following the passing of the articles of impeachment, regardless of whether or not he/she is ultimately convicted or acquitted in the Senate.

- **COMPARATIVE** UK prime ministers can theoretically be removed through an impeachment process similar to that operating in the USA. In January 2006, for example, General Sir Michael Rose, one-time commander of UN forces in Bosnia, argued that Tony Blair should be impeached for leading Britain into war in Iraq under false pretences (i.e. the supposed presence of weapons of mass destruction). The last impeachment in Britain concerned Lord Melville, who was impeached in 1806 for corrupt misuse of public funds.

imperial presidency: a phrase originating in the 1960s but entering common usage as a result of the publication in 1973 of Arthur Schlesinger Jr.'s book, *The Imperial Presidency*, which refers to the expansion in the scope and extent of presidential power in the USA.

- This growth in presidential power had accompanied the massive expansion in the size and scope of the federal government that had come in the wake of the *Great Depression*. See *New Deal*.

- Schlesinger argued that a gradual expansion in the power of the presidency since the *ratification* of the *Constitution*, had gained pace in the twentieth century as the president found ways of circumventing the constitutional checks on his *power.*

- **e.g.** the way in which successive presidents have used *executive agreements* as a means of avoiding the two-thirds *Senate* backing needed to ratify formal *treaties* negotiated by the president.

- **TIP** Such fluidity in the relationship between the *executive* and the *legislature* was possible because, as *Richard Neustadt* recognised, the Constitution had established a system of 'separated institutions sharing powers', as opposed to a full *separation of powers.*

implied powers: in contrast to those *enumerated powers* explicitly granted to the US *Congress* in the *Constitution*, the implied powers are those which are needed in order for the *legislature* to carry out its assigned roles.

- The implied powers are rooted primarily in the *'necessary and proper clause'* (or 'elastic clause') found in Article 1 of the Constitution.

- **TIP** The term can also be used with regard to the unwritten *emergency powers* that flow from the president's constitutional roles of commander-in-chief and chief executive.

impoundment: see *Budget and Impoundment Control Act (1974).*

incumbency: in US politics an incumbent is the current holder of the political office in question. Incumbency refers to the rate at which those already in office are re-elected to their positions (i.e. high or low levels of incumbency).

- **e.g.** Incumbency rates are high in the US *Congress*. In the 2004 congressional elections 97.8% of those who sought re-election in the House were returned as were 91.6% of those incumbent Senators who were up for re-election.

- **TIP** Some argue that high levels of incumbency are attributable to the greater levels of campaign finance that such candidates attract. Others maintain that incumbency reflects satisfaction with the work that sitting members have done for their states and *districts.*

Independent Regulatory Commission (IRC): an agency that is beyond the direct control of the *legislature* or the *executive* and is most often charged with the task of regulating an aspect of industrial or commercial life, e.g. see *Federal Trade Commission.*

- Though IRCs are supposed to be independent, the *president* and *Congress* can exercise influence over such agencies. *Eisenhower*'s assistant, Sherman Adams, admitted to secretly asking commissioners to resign, and there are close informal links between the IRCs and the presidential staff.

- **TIP** IRCs have the power to establish and enforce statutory regulations within their sphere of operations. This quasi-legislative and quasi-judicial function led M. J. C. Vile to describe them as the 'headless fourth branch' of the US government.

independent voter: any voter who is not a registered supporter of a political party.

- Supporters of *third parties* are often also categorised as independent voters in US polls.
- ▨ *TIP* It is often mistakenly believed that the proportion of voters identifying themselves as independent increased between 1980 and 2004. Though the percentage of voters who identified strongly with a party did decline during this period, the number who regarded themselves as wholly independent actually fell.
- ▨ *e.g.* Whereas the percentage of voters identifying themselves as independent on a 'three-point scale' (i.e. Democrat, Independent, or Republican) was 13% in 1980, it fell to 12% in 2000 and 10% in 2004.

Indiana: the nineteenth state; joined the *Union* in 1816.

individualism: said to be one of the defining characteristics of US political culture, an approach that stresses the importance of individual rights and liberty over the supposed collective interests of those living under a given state.

- Although individualism appears to suggest selfishness, its advocates argue that the common good will ultimately be served by citizens pursuing their own ends. This is because individuals ultimately recognise the benefits that they themselves will gain from moderating certain aspects of their own behaviour.
- ▨ *TIP* Individualism can be contrasted with approaches that are more collectivist or communitarian in nature.

initiative: a mechanism by which citizens in around 20 US states can force a *referendum* by collecting a pre-determined number of signatures from registered voters.

- Initiatives can normally be used to change regular state law or amend the state constitution.
- No provision exists for nationwide initiatives in the USA.
- Initiatives are sometimes referred to as 'propositions'.
- ▨ *e.g.* See *Proposition 13 (1978)*.
- ▨ *COMPARATIVE* No provision for initiatives exists in the UK. Those referendums held have always been at times and on issues set by the government of the day.

interest group: often simply used as an alternative to the phrase *pressure group* in the USA. The term can be defined more tightly as a group that aims to serve the direct interests of its members, i.e. a 'sectional' as opposed to a 'cause' pressure group.

- ▨ *e.g.* the *American Association of Retired Persons (AARP)*.

Internal Revenue Service (IRS): a bureau of the US Treasury Department concerned with collecting taxes and enforcing revenue laws.

- ▨ *COMPARATIVE* The Inland Revenue is the UK equivalent to the IRS.

invisible primary: the interval between candidates declaring an intention to run in a presidential election and the date of the first actual contests of the primary season, the Iowa *caucus* and the *New Hampshire primary.*

● The length of the invisible primary is dependent upon the date on which candidates declare, e.g. *George W. Bush* declared more than 7 months before the first primary in 2000 and *Hillary Clinton* and *Barack Obama* had both declared for the 2008 presidential election by February 2007.

● During this pre-primary stage candidates seek to gain nationwide name-recognition and also attract the level of campaign finance that will be crucial if they are to do well in the early caucuses and primary elections.

▓ *e.g.* In 2004 *Howard Dean* had, by his own admission, spent most of the $50 million that he had raised during the invisible primary in an effort to win the Iowa caucus.

▓ *TIP* Some argue that there is now a kind of 'permanent election' for the presidency; where one electoral cycle begins almost as soon as the previous one has ended. This has long been the case in respect of the *House of Representatives.*

Iowa: the twenty-ninth state; joined the *Union* in 1846.

Iran-Contra affair: a scandal involving the secret sale of arms to Iran — in violation of an international embargo — and the subsequent use of the monies generated to fund the anti-communist Contras in Nicaragua.

● President *Reagan* wanted to fund the Contras, a right-wing guerilla organisation that was fighting against the Sandinista-led communist government in Nicaragua.

● In 1982 *Congress* had amended the Defense Appropriations Bill in such a way as to bar Reagan from funding the Contras. See also *pork-barrelled bill.*

● Iran was at war with Iraq and needed to arm itself. Iran was also said to have influence over a number of paramilitary groups holding American hostages in the Middle East.

▓ *TIP* The Iran-Contra affair led to the formation of a special joint investigative committee in Congress, the Iran-Contra Committee. This committee heard evidence from many of the key figures accused of being involved in the trade — including *National Security Council* aide Colonel Oliver North and Reagan himself — without ever clarifying exactly what had transpired.

iron triangle: a term applied to the close three-way relationship that can develop between the dominant national *pressure group* in a particular field, the relevant *congressional committee,* and the *executive agency* or bureau of the *executive department* that has responsibility for the area of policy in question.

● As such relationships are formed, other interested parties are excluded from the 'policy-loop'.

● Iron triangles can have the effect of undermining the effectiveness of any regulatory function the government agency in question may have.

- **e.g.** The Military Industrial Complex (MIC), recognised by *Dwight Eisenhower* in 1950s, is probably the best known iron triangle.
- **TIP** Iron triangles are closely associated with notions of *clientelism* and *agency capture*.

IRC: see *Independent Regulatory Commission.*

IRS: see *Internal Revenue Service.*

issue advocacy: normally used in reference to the campaigns organised by *interest groups* in support of, or opposition to, one or more candidates in an election.

- Issue advocacy was widely seen as a way of circumventing the restrictions on direct contributions to candidates' campaigns (i.e. *hard money*) set out in the *Federal Election Campaign Act (1974).*
- The *Bipartisan Campaign Finance Reform Act (BCRA) (2002)* restricted the use of electioneering ads by companies, corporations, and *unions*. Under this Act, ads featuring the likenesses or names of candidates were banned within 30 days of a *primary election* and 60 days of a general election. *Political action committees (PACs)* were unaffected by these changes as they operate under the rules already governing hard money contributions.
- BCRA (2002) also required 'non-corporate or non-union persons or entities that spend in excess of $10,000 on electioneering communications' to provide full disclosure regarding their income and expenditure.

Ivy League: refers to a group of eight elite institutions of higher education located in the northeast of the USA.

- **e.g.** The Ivy League comprises Brown University, Columbia University, Cornell University, Dartmouth College, Harvard University, Princeton University, University of Pennsylvania, and Yale University.
- **TIP** Graduates of such institutions are statistically over-represented in the professions and in higher political office. Both of the major parties' candidates in the 2004 presidential election, *George W. Bush* and *John Kerry*, were graduates of Yale.
- **COMPARATIVE** Some draw comparisons between the Ivy League in the USA and Oxbridge in the UK.

Jackson, Andrew (1767–1845): the seventh US *president*, 1829–37.

Jackson, Jesse (1941–): Democrat politician, Baptist minister and civil rights campaigner, he was a candidate for the Democratic presidential nomination in 1984 and 1988.

- In the 1980s Jackson was active in programmes designed to encourage black *voter registration* and increased *turnout* amongst minority groups.

- Jackson favoured creating a 'rainbow coalition', uniting ethnic minority voters and white citizens from lower income groups in pursuit of progressive, left-of-centre policies.

Jefferson, Thomas (1743–1826): the third US *president*, 1801–09.

- Jefferson was the main author of the *Declaration of Independence*, which was adopted by the Second *Continental Congress* in 1776.

- He is widely regarded as one of the most influential of the *Founding Fathers* who attended the *Philadelphia Constitution Convention* in 1787.

Jeffords, James (1934–): a former member of the US *Senate*, representing Vermont, who effectively handed control of the Senate to the Democrats when he left the Republican Party to become an independent Senator in 2001.

Johnson, Andrew (1808–75): the seventeenth US *president*, 1865–69.

- Johnson became president as a result of the assassination of *Abraham Lincoln* in 1865.

- His willingness to use his veto to block civil rights reforms helped to placate former Confederate states and ease their path back into the *Union* though it also had the effect of upsetting many radical Republicans.

- A deterioration in relations between Johnson and the *Congress* resulted in his *impeachment* by the *House of Representatives* in 1868. He was only acquitted in the *Senate* by a single vote, with the 35 to 19 margin in favour of impeachment falling just short of the two-thirds majority that would have seen him removed from office.

Johnson, Lyndon Baines ('LBJ') (1908–73): a one-time member of the *House of Representatives* and later *majority leader* for the Democrats in the US *Senate*.

Vice-president from 1961–63, Johnson served as the thirty-sixth US *president* between 1963 and 1969 following the assassination of *John F. Kennedy*.

- On the domestic front, Johnson is best remembered for his *Great Society* programme.
- His foreign policy was dominated by his decision to extend US involvement in Vietnam by committing increasingly large numbers of ground troops to the conflict. The escalation of the war and rising US casualties contributed to Johnson's decision not to seek re-election in 1968. He died in 1973.
- **e.g.** A number of important Acts were introduced during Johnson's time in office. These include the *Civil Rights Act (1964)* and the *Voting Rights Act (1965)*.

judicial activism: a term arising from the US *Supreme Court*'s extensive and controversial use of *judicial review*, particularly during the 1950s and 1960s.

- Under Chief Justice *Earl Warren*, the Court used its powers of review to push back society's frontiers.
- **e.g.** See *Brown* v *Board of Education, Topeka (1954)* on segregation, *Griswold* v *Connecticut (1965)* on access to contraception, and *Miranda* v *Arizona (1966)* on the rights of the accused.
- **TIP** Even during periods of supposed judicial activism, the Court rarely makes decisions that are diametrically opposed to the wishes of the *president, Congress* and the public at large. When it has done so (e.g. in declaring elements of the *New Deal* programme invalid) it has come under acute pressure.
- **COMPARATIVE** In the UK, the term judicial activism has been used with reference to the way in which the courts have interpreted the Human Rights Act (1998) so as to challenge elements of the government's anti-terrorism strategy, specifically the indefinite detention of terrorist suspects allowed under the Anti-terrorism, Crime and Security Act (2001).

judicial restraint: the courts' natural inclination to accept the principle of *stare decisis* and follow the *precedents* set out in previous cases.

- **e.g.** Though the Court has allowed certain limits on access to *abortion*, it has always stopped short of overturning *Roe* v *Wade (1973)*.

judicial review: the convention by which the US *Supreme Court* may void any actions or statutes, whether by state or federal government, where it determines that such actions or statutes come into conflict with the *Constitution*.

- The power of judicial review was not explicitly set out in Article 3 of the US Constitution. The Court is said to have 'discovered' this power in a number of landmark cases early in the nineteenth century.
- **e.g.** The case of *Marbury* v *Madison (1803)* is generally said to mark the point at which the Court's power of judicial review was first established.
- **TIP** The style of judicial review present in the USA is rooted in the fact that regular statute is inferior to the Constitution and that it can therefore be tested against it.

▪ *COMPARATIVE* In the UK, the principle of parliamentary sovereignty and the primacy of statute law have greatly limited the courts' powers of judicial review.

judiciary: a collective term referring to the courts, tribunals, judges, magistrates and other adjudicators concerned with the application of the law and the administration of justice within a state.

Justice Department: first established in 1870, 1 of 15 US *executive departments* in existence in 2007.

● The head of the Justice Department has *cabinet* rank and is referred to as the attorney general.

▪ *e.g.* In 2007 the attorney general was Alberto Gonzales.

▪ *COMPARATIVE* In 2007 it was announced that the Department of Constitutional Affairs would be taking on a number of new responsibilities and would be renamed the Justice Department as part of the planned reorganisation of the Home Office.

Kansas: the thirty-fourth state; joined the *Union* in 1861.

Keating Five: the five US Senators investigated as a result of the collapse of Charles Keating's Lincoln Savings and Loans Association, one of many such institutions that collapsed in the 1980s.

- Charles Keating had been investigated by federal regulators in connection with the collapse.
- The Senate Ethics Committee investigated five Senators accused of improperly interfering in the investigation into Charles Keating. The Keating Five were also said to have collectively received more than $1 million in campaign contributions from Keating.

■ *e.g.* Four of the five — Senators DeConcini, Glenn, McCain and Riegle — were cited for questionable conduct — the fifth, Senator Cranston, was censured for reprehensible conduct.

Kennedy, Anthony (1936–): an associate justice of the US *Supreme Court*, appointed by *Ronald Reagan* in 1988.

- There was a 237-day gap between the resignation of Kennedy's predecessor on the bench, Associate Justice Lewis Powell, and Kennedy's own confirmation. This resulted from the *Senate*'s rejection of Reagan's first nominee, *Robert Bork*, and the withdrawal of his second nominee, *Douglas Ginsburg*.
- Though Reagan appointed Kennedy believing him to be a reliable conservative voice on the bench, he has in fact been closer to the centre, being the crucial swing vote in a number of cases and siding with the liberal wing on others.

■ *e.g.* In *Romer* v *Evans* (1996), Kennedy voted with the liberals in the Court to rule that Colorado's Amendment 2, which forbade laws protecting homosexuals from discrimination, was *unconstitutional*. The decision was opposed by conservative Justices *William H. Rehnquist, Antonin Scalia* and *Clarence Thomas*.

Kennedy, Edward (1932–): *Democratic Party* politician and long-serving member of the US *Senate*. The youngest brother of the late *John F. Kennedy* (assassinated in 1963) and Senator *Robert F. Kennedy* (assassinated in 1968).

- Long expected to follow his brothers' example in running for the White House, Kennedy's reputation suffered as a result of events at *Chappaquiddick*.

- In 1980 Kennedy's supporters failed in an attempt to remove the Democratic Party Convention's first-ballot pledge. Had they succeeded, he would have been able to win the party's presidential nomination without having secured victory in the *primaries*.

Kennedy, John F. (1917–63): the thirty-fifth US *president*. He served from 1961 until his assassination by Lee Harvey Oswald in 1963.

- Kennedy's domestic policy came under the umbrella of his *New Frontier* programme, some of which was later assimilated into *Lyndon Johnson*'s *Great Society* programme.

- In foreign policy, Kennedy's short term in office was dominated by the Bay of Pigs fiasco, and the Cold War crises surrounding the building of the Berlin Wall (1961) and the siting of Soviet missiles on Cuba (see *Cuban Missile Crisis*).

Kennedy, Robert (1925–68): one-time US attorney general (1961–64) and later US Senator. Competed for the *Democratic Party* nomination in the 1968 presidential election but was assassinated shortly after securing victory over rival Eugene McCarthy in the California primary.

- He is best remembered for his work in advancing the cause of Black Civil Rights during his time as attorney general

Kentucky: the fifteenth state; joined the *Union* in 1792.

Kerry, John (1943–): decorated Vietnam veteran, US Senator for Massachusetts, and *Democratic Party* candidate in the 2004 presidential election. Kerry was defeated by the incumbent Republican President *George W. Bush*.

King, Martin Luther (1929–68): a Baptist minister and high profile leader of the Black Civil Rights movement in the USA. He was the youngest man to be awarded the Nobel Peace Prize. He was assassinated in Memphis, Tennessee in 1968.

- King was closely associated with the promotion of non-violent forms of protest.

- *e.g.* the use of peaceful protest marches involving women and children in Birmingham, Alabama. See *Eugene 'Bull' Connor*.

King, Rodney (1965–): a black American citizen, whose violent arrest at the hands of the Los Angeles Police Department (LAPD) was filmed by a chance bystander.

- King's case was seen as evidence of a more widespread problem of racism within the LAPD.

- The surprise acquittal in state court of the four officers charged with the use of excessive force in King's arrest sparked the Los Angeles riots in 1992.

- The officers were later tried and convicted under federal law in a *federal court*.

Kissinger, Henry (1923–): a German-born US *national security advisor* (NSA) and later secretary of state under President *Richard Nixon*. He retained the latter role under Nixon's successor, President *Gerald Ford*.

- Kissinger played a key role in expanding the role of the *National Security Council* (NSC) under President Richard Nixon.

- As NSA, Kissinger effectively excluded the then Secretary of State William Rogers from foreign policy matters. Kissinger retained the role of NSA when he took on the role of secretary of state from 1973.
- In 1973 Kissinger won the Nobel Peace Prize for his work in bringing an end to the *Vietnam War*. He also gained plaudits for his use of 'shuttle diplomacy' to bring about a ceasefire in the Arab-Israeli War (1973).

■ *TIP* Often regarded as one of the 'best presidents that American never had', Kissinger was prevented from running for the White House as a result of the fact that he was not a natural born citizen.

kitchen cabinet: a small inner group of presidential advisors. The term originated in the meetings between President *Andrew Jackson* and his friends in the White House kitchen.

■ *COMPARATIVE* In the UK, the increased use of kitchen cabinets (sometimes called 'inner cabinets') and bilateral meetings has accompanied the decline in the full cabinet as a collective decision-making body.

Korean War: a conflict that resulted from North Korea's decision to invade the South in 1950. It ended in a stalemate (a ceasefire), as opposed to a formal peace treaty, in 1953.

- Korea had been divided along the 38th Parallel following its liberation from Japanese forces at the end of the Second World War.
- Communist North Korea, led by Kim Il Sung, invaded the South in 1950 and the United Nations Security Council authorised a military response thereafter.
- A US-led United Nations force liberated the South and pushed forward towards the border between North Korea and China. Chinese forces then crossed the Yalu River into North Korea and pushed south.
- The ceasefire that ultimately brought an end to the fighting left the border where it had been at the start of the war, on the 38th Parallel. This demarcation line remains one of the most heavily militarised borders in the world.

■ *e.g.* Over 54,000 US troops were killed in the war, with a further 100,000 injured. Chinese and Korean casualties, both military and civilian, probably totalled more than 2 million, a direct result of the extensive US bombing campaign.

■ *TIP* The war was one of the key issues in the 1952 presidential election campaign, where the ultimately victorious Republican candidate *Dwight Eisenhower* announced that he would 'go to Korea' to resolve the conflict.

■ *COMPARATIVE* The UK contributed troops to the UN army sent to liberate South Korea.

Koresh, David (1959–93): see *Branch Davidians.*

K-Street: sometimes referred to as the 'K-Street corridor', a major street in Washington DC on which the offices of a large number of lobby groups and think-tanks are located.

Kyoto Protocol: an agreement concluded at an intergovernmental meeting on climate change held in the Japanese city of Kyoto in 1997.

- The Protocol was originally signed by 38 countries.
- Signatories agreed to reduce their atmospheric CO_2 emissions by an average of just over 5% by 2012, as compared to 1990 figures.
- The impact of the agreement was hampered by the fact that the United States under *George W. Bush* unilaterally withdrew from the Protocol. At the time the USA was said to be responsible for around one-quarter of global CO_2 emissions.
- **TIP** The US withdrawal from the agreement was widely seen as evidence of America pursuing its own short-term economic interests over broader environmental concerns. The US government defended its decision by questioning some of the scientific evidence behind theories of global warming.
- **COMPARATIVE** The UK is a signatory to the Kyoto Protocol and is working towards meeting its 2012 target on CO_2 emissions.

lame duck: a term traditionally applied to a *president* who though defeated in a November election, remains in office until the following January. It is also used to describe a president who is set to leave office having served the maximum of two 4-year terms permitted under the *Twenty-Second Amendment* (1951).

● A lame-duck president is said to lack the mandate necessary to make major changes in policy or to fill important vacancies.

● Lame-duck presidents often experience more problematic relations with *Congress*.

▥ *e.g.* *George H. W. Bush* was a lame-duck president from the time of his election defeat in November 1992, until January 1993, when *Bill Clinton* was sworn into office.

▥ *TIP* Since the *ratification* of the Twenty-Second Amendment in 1951 it has become common for the term to be applied to a president who appears to be struggling at any point in their second term, e.g. Bill Clinton in the wake of the *Monica Lewinsky* scandal.

▥ *COMPARATIVE* Many commentators characterised UK Prime Minister Tony Blair as a lame-duck following his announcement in 2005 that he would not be leading the Labour Party into a fourth successive general election campaign.

LCV: see *League of Conservation Voters*.

League of Conservation Voters (LCV): an issue-based US *pressure group* that seeks to encourage the adoption of more environmentally friendly policies.

● The LVC actively campaigns in favour of candidates with good environmental credentials.

▥ *e.g.* The group is known for its National Environmental Scorecard, which rates members of the US *Congress* according to their voting-records on environmental issues. Its 'Dirty Dozen' list names the 12 *Congressmen* with the worst records; the 'Environmental Champions' list celebrates the best.

Lee v Weisman (1992): a case in which the US *Supreme Court* ruled that it was *unconstitutional* for a public school to include prayers read by a religious leader at a graduation ceremony as it violated the Establishment Clause of the *First Amendment*.

legislative process: collectively, the steps by which formal policy proposals become law.

- In the USA the legislative process involves both chambers of *Congress*, the *House of Representatives* and the *Senate*, which hold co-equal legislative power. The president then has a limited power of veto over measures passing the *legislature*.

- **TIP** In reality the most significant step in the US legislative process is the committee stage. Significantly, US *standing committees* deal with legislation ahead of the 'second reading'.

- **COMPARATIVE** In the UK, the legislative process is normally dominated by the party of government, i.e. the majority party in the Commons. Far from being a co-equal legislative chamber, the Lords has traditionally been expected to be more of a revising chamber, a role reinforced by statute (e.g. the Parliament Acts) and convention (e.g. the Salisbury Doctrine).

legislature: the branch of government concerned with formally making law.

- The USA, in common with many liberal democracies, has a *bicameral* legislature consisting of the *House of Representatives* and the *Senate*.

- Forty-nine of the fifty US states had bicameral legislatures in 2007. The fiftieth, *Nebraska*, has adopted a unicameral model.

- **COMPARATIVE** The fact that the key figures in the UK government are drawn from the legislature (most often the Commons) means that the separation between executive and legislature is less distinct than in the USA. The UK is said to have a fusion of powers as opposed to a *separation of powers*.

legitimacy: the existence of a collective confidence in a government's right to govern amongst a nation's citizenry, i.e. the public has faith in the institutions and processes by which it is governed.

- In its political usage the term has its roots in the work of the German sociologist Max Weber.

- **TIP** Legitimacy is closely linked to the concept of *authority*.

legitimisation: a process designed to afford a government or other authority a degree of *legitimacy*.

- Though governments most often gain legitimacy through free and fair elections, devices such as *referendums* can also be used in order to legitimise a particular course of action.

- **e.g.** In the US state of California a referendum is required in order to approve, and thereby legitimise, any change to the state's constitution.

- **COMPARATIVE** The referendums held in Scotland and Wales in 1997 played a part in legitimising the devolution programme approved by parliament, and earlier set out in the Labour Party's 1997 general election manifesto.

Lemon Law: a US law that affords consumers a degree of protection when buying used automobiles.

- The term is a nick-name that can refer to any one of a number of similar Acts operating within individual US states or to the federal Lemon Law. It has its origins in the fact that defective cars are referred to as 'lemons' in the USA.
- **e.g.** Though the federal Lemon Law, the Magnuson-Moss Warranty Act, protects citizens across all US states, the laws enacted within some individual states afford an even greater degree of protection. Lemon Laws in some states have been extended to cover not only automobiles but any mechanical item.
- **TIP** In the USA, *pressure groups* representing the used-car industry have been active in trying to block and limit such measures. In 1997, for example, the US Consumers' Union reported that NADA (the National Automobile Dealers' Association) successfully lobbied to have the *House of Representatives* pass a bill (336 votes to 72) that would allow used-car dealers to sell cars over 7 years old without full disclosure of the vehicle's history and would also limit the rights of consumers to gain compensation if they discovered that they had been sold a 'lemon'. It was subsequently reported that 90% of House Members who had received $4,000 or more in campaign contributions from NADA or related *interest groups* voted for the bill, whereas only 32% of those receiving no money or contributions below $4,000 had done so.
- **COMPARATIVE** In the UK, the purchase of second-hand goods is often said to be covered by the phrase *caveat emptor* ('let the buyer beware').

Lewinsky, Monica (1973–): a former White House intern who gained notoriety as a result of her intimate relationship with then President *Bill Clinton*, an 'affair' commonly referred to as the 'Lewinsky Scandal' or 'Monicagate'.

- On legal advice Clinton denied having 'sexual relations with that woman'. Subsequent revelations regarding precisely what had gone on between the president and Lewinsky in the Oval Office saw this narrow legalistic definition of 'sexual relations' widely ridiculed.
- Clinton was ultimately *impeached* over his attempt to mislead the commission investigating the affair.
- **TIP** Monicagate and the impeachment process that followed cast a shadow over Bill Clinton's second term. Some argue that it also made it difficult for *Al Gore* to make full use of 'the Clinton factor' in the 2000 presidential election.

liberal democracy: commonly refers to the modern western style of democracy that incorporates free and fair elections with a belief in the importance of certain core rights and responsibilities.

Libertarian Party: founded in 1971, one of the larger permanent *third parties* in the USA.

- The party favours greater emphasis on individual liberties and laissez-faire economics.
- **e.g.** In 2007 the party had over 200,000 registered voters and held in excess of 500 locally elected offices.

Lieberman, Joseph (1942–): a one-time *Democratic Party* member of the US Senate, Lieberman was vice-presidential candidate to *Al Gore* in the party's failed bid to win the presidential election in 2000.

● Lieberman continued serving in the Senate following victory for the Republican Bush-Cheney ticket in 2000.

● In 2006 Lieberman was defeated in the primary election for his Senate seat yet went on to run and win as an independent. In January 2007 Lieberman entered the 110th *Congress* as an 'Independent Democrat', although he still sat with his former colleagues in the Democratic *caucus* in the Senate.

▨ *TIP* Lieberman's loss in the 2006 primary election for his Senate seat was widely seen as a result of the *Democratic National Committee* favouring a rival Democrat in the contest.

limited government: the principle that the size and scope of central government should be limited to that which is necessary only for the common good of the people.

● In the USA, limited government is synonymous with ideas of 'small government' and opposition to the kind of 'big government' interventionism that was common around the time of the *New Deal*.

● 'Small government' is in turn synonymous with 'state rights' under the *reserved powers* protected under the *Tenth Amendment*.

▨ *TIP* A belief in the principle of limited government is said to be one of the defining characteristics of US *political culture*.

Lincoln, Abraham (1809–65): the sixteenth US *president*, 1861–65. He was assassinated by actor John Wilkes Booth whilst attending a theatre in Washington DC in 1865.

● Born in Kentucky, Lincoln lived out the *American Dream* of going 'from the log cabin to the White House'.

● He is famous for his leadership of the *Union* during the American *Civil War* (1861–65).

● He is also known for his long-term opposition to the expansion of *slavery* from southern states to the North, for his Emancipation Proclamation (1863), and for overseeing the passage of the *Thirteenth Amendment* (1865), which abolished slavery throughout the USA.

line-item veto: a *president* possessing a line-item veto would be able to delete individual lines or items from a piece of legislation before giving it his or her approval.

● This is different from the power of veto granted to the US president under the *Constitution*, where he is required to either sign or veto the entire bill (see also *pocket veto*).

● The Line Item Veto Act (1996) came into effect in 1997. It granted the president a form of line-item veto by allowing him to delete the amounts allocated to specific items in spending bills within 5 days of a bill being signed.

- *Bill Clinton* used this power on 82 occasions between August 1997 and June 1988, cutting over $300 million from the *federal budget*.
- In June 1998 the *Supreme Court* ruled the line-item veto *unconstitutional* in the case of *Clinton* v *New York City* (6:3).

■ *TIP* The Republican-controlled *Congress* had passed the Line Item Veto Act (1996) in the hope that President Clinton would use it to remove the irrelevant *riders* (amendments) that House Members often add to bills as a means of securing benefits for their *districts* or states (see also *pork-barrelling* and *log-rolling*).

lobbying: an attempt to exert influence on the policy-making process, normally by means of informal contacts between professional *lobbyists* and one or more legislators.

- The term has its origins in the 'lobby' areas within *Congress*, where professional lobbyists are more easily able to meet with legislators.

■ *COMPARATIVE* In the UK, the 'Cash for Questions' scandal involved monies said to have been paid by Mohamed Al Fayed to the then Tatton MP Neil Hamilton, who was working for the lobbying firm Ian Greer Associates.

lobbyist: an individual professionally engaged in *lobbying*, whether in pursuit of an interest close to his/her own heart or, more often, on behalf of another individual or group.

- Most *pressure groups* employ professional lobbyists, either permanently or on an ad hoc basis as a part of specific campaigns.
- Many of the most influential professional lobbyists work for agencies and companies based in Washington's *K-Street*.
- Former members of *Congress* often take up paid positions within lobbying firms. See *revolving-door syndrome*.

locality rule: existing under state law in a number of the larger US states, a requirement that those serving as elected members of the US *House of Representatives* should be resident not only in the state they represent, as demanded by the US *Constitution*, but also in the congressional *district* from which they are returned.

■ *COMPARATIVE* In the UK, there is no requirement for MPs to be resident in the constituencies that they represent in the House of Commons. In the 2005 general election, for example, none of the three major party candidates contesting the Harborough seat were resident in the constituency.

Locke, John (1632–1704): a seventeenth-century English philosopher famous for helping to develop ideas of 'popular consent' and the 'social contract' later popularised by writers such as the Genevan philosopher *Jean Jacques Rousseau*.

- Locke argued that a people had an absolute right to overthrow any state that operated without the consent of those it governed.
- Locke's ideas were said to have been a major influence on those who led the 'American Revolution' (or *American War of Independence*).

■ *e.g.* Locke's influence is reflected in the *Declaration of Independence* issued by the Second *Continental Congress* in 1776.

log-rolling (or 'horse-trading')**:** describing the way in which members of the US *Congress* trade their support on different bills in order to gain the safe passage of measures that benefit each member's *district* or state.

● Log-rolling is closely associated with pork-barrelling.

loose constructionists: those justices who place emphasis on inferences (see *penumbras*) or previous *precedent* when interpreting the law or constitutional passage at the heart of a particular case.

● Loose constructionist US *Supreme Court* justices are said to 'read between the lines' of the US *Constitution* in order to establish whether or not individual Acts of regulations at state or federal level should be struck down or allowed to stand.

● Loose constructionists (such as *Earl Warren*) can be contrasted with *strict constructionists* (such as *Antonin Scalia*) who look to base their rulings on the actual text of the passage of the Constitution in question. Such strict constructionists are often said to be concerned with establishing the 'original intent' of the *Founding Fathers*.

■ *e.g.* the way in which the US Supreme Court used passages in the Constitution (the *First, Fourth, Fifth* and *Ninth Amendments*) to establish a 'zone of privacy' which guaranteed a right to contraception (see *Griswold* v *Connecticut, 1965*) and *abortion* (see *Roe* v *Wade, 1973*).

■ *TIP* Loose constructionism is most closely associated with the *judicial activism* of the Warren Court between 1954 and 1969.

Lott, Trent (1941–): a Republican and member of the US *Senate* serving Mississippi. One-time Senate *majority leader* and briefly minority leader following *James Jeffords*'s defection from 'Republican' to 'Independent' in 2001. He was elected Senate minority *whip* in November 2006 following the *Democratic Party*'s successes in the *mid-term elections*.

● Like many Republicans returned from southern states (see *Strom Thurmond, Jesse Helms*), Lott's comments have often provoked controversy.

■ *e.g.* Lott was forced to resign from the post of Senate minority leader in December 2002, following remarks he made at Senator Strom Thurmond's 100th birthday party. Lott had reportedly expressed regret that the one-time segregationist Thurmond had not been successful when running as an independent in the 1948 presidential election.

Louisiana: the eighteenth state; joined the *Union* in 1812.

***Lynch* v *Donnelly* (1984):** a case in which the US *Supreme Court* ruled that a Christmas display in the City of Pawtucket, Rhode Island, which contained Santa Claus and a Christmas tree, did not violate the Establishment Clause of the *First Amendment*.

machine politics: refers to the almost total control that one or other of the main US parties came to exercise in some US cities by the 1950s.

- In these cities the party machine, often headed by a single boss, would oversee a *spoils system*, using their patronage to reward key party workers and other supporters with government contracts and paid positions.
- Machine politics is synonymous with the image of *fat cats* concluding deals in *smoke-filled rooms*.
- These all-powerful party machines were often very geographically focused and intensely territorial.
- ▉ *e.g.* According to H. G. Nicholas, the Brooklyn Democrats' slogan, 'the tiger shall not cross the bridge', was aimed not at Republicans but at their Democratic neighbours across the river in Manhattan.
- ▉ *TIP* Though machine politics is still said to operate in some areas, Anthony Bennett argues that the days of the 'cigar chomping, fedora-hatted political boss' probably ended with the death of Chicago mayor Richard Daley in 1976.

Madison, James (1751–1836): the fourth US *president*, 1809–17.

- Prior to being president Madison had been one of the most influential *Founding Fathers* involved in drafting the new *Constitution* in 1787.
- Madison was one of the main advocates of the system of *checks and balances* that was eventually *entrenched* in the US system.
- He is widely credited with undertaking much of the work that eventually resulted in the drafting of the *Bill of Rights*.

Maine: the twenty-third state; joined the *Union* in 1820.

- Along with Nebraska, Maine is one of the states that does not award its *Electoral College* votes on a winner-takes-all basis. See *Maine System*.

Maine System: a means of apportioning *Electoral College* votes, used by Nebraska and Maine.

- Under this system a presidential candidate wins one Electoral College vote for each congressional *district* they carry (under a simple plurality system) plus a bonus of two Electoral College votes for being the state-wide winner.
- Some argue that the adoption of the Maine System by all states would provide a fairer method for apportioning Electoral College votes as it would make it

harder for a candidate who lost the popular vote nationally to secure a victory in the Electoral College. This is not necessarily the case, however.

■ *e.g.* Anthony Bennett has calculated that the nation-wide adoption of the Maine System would have resulted in an even less proportionate result in the 2000 presidential election than occurred under the arrangements currently in place. Bush would have won by 38 Electoral College votes as opposed to the actual margin of 4.

majority and minority leaders: the individuals who coordinate the efforts of each party within the *House* and the *Senate*. Such leadership figures hold a broad responsibility for leading their party's *caucus* within each chamber.

● The majority and minority leaders in each chamber work closely with the majority and minority *whips* in order to try and enforce party discipline.

■ *e.g.* In April 2007 the majority leader in the House was Steny Hoyer (Democrat, Maryland) and the minority leader was John Boehner (Republican, Ohio). In the Senate the majority leader was Harry Reid (Democrat, Nevada) and the minority leader was Mitch McConnell (Republican, Kentucky).

■ *TIP* The majority leader in the House of Representatives also has to work closely with the House *Speaker* who will come from the same congressional caucus and be a partisan figure, unlike his/her UK counterpart.

majority-minority district (or majority-minority state): normally refers to a situation where the majority of a congressional district's (or state's) population differs in terms of *ethnicity* from the majority in the national population.

● The term is most often where a *district* (or state) is majority non-white; hence it is said to be majority-minority.

■ *e.g.* Around 80% of the US population define themselves as white, whereas only around 27% of those in Hawaii fall into this category. Hawaii is, therefore, a majority-minority state. Washington DC is also majority-minority; with 57% *African-American*.

■ *COMPARATIVE* It has been predicted that Leicester will become the first majority-minority UK city by 2030.

mandate: the right of an elected government to carry into law those policies that formed the basis of its manifesto in the preceding election.

● The vagueness of US party *platforms* and the *candidate-centred* nature of campaigns undermines the notion of the mandate.

● The fact that the *president* and *Congress* are elected independently of one another also creates a situation in which the *executive* and the *legislature* may have opposing mandates, particularly where they are controlled by different parties.

■ *e.g.* Clinton was unable to persuade a Democrat-controlled Congress to pass his *healthcare reform* programme in 1993 and 1994. The Republicans then took control of Congress in 1995 having secured a popular mandate for their *Contract with America* programme in the 1994 *mid-term elections*.

■ **COMPARATIVE** The fact that the UK executive is drawn from the legislature makes it easier for the party in government to deliver on the promises made in its manifesto.

manipulative theory (re: the media): the belief that the mass *media* is controlled by an elite that uses it with the sole purpose of preserving the status quo and, therefore, its own position.

● The theory states that serious news stories that have the ability to embarrass the elite are suppressed in favour of celebrity trivia. As Billy Bragg wrote in his song, *It says here*, '…If this does not reflect your view you should understand that those who own the papers also own this land and they'd rather you believe in *Coronation Street* capers, in the war for circulation it sells newspapers…'.

■ **e.g.** Under manipulative theory, New Labour's re-branding under Tony Blair might have had the effect of making the party more acceptable to the dominant elite and, therefore, worthy of support in the face of a divided and unstable Conservative Party. David Cameron's rise might be seen in a similar light.

Marbury v Madison (1803): a landmark case in which the US *Supreme Court* was said to have 'discovered' its power of *judicial review*.

● The case concerned *Thomas Jefferson*'s unwillingness to honour an appointment made by his predecessor in the White House, *John Adams*.

● The appointee, William Marbury, petitioned against Secretary of State *James Madison*, the man whom Jefferson had ordered to withhold Marbury's commission.

■ **TIP** The significance of the case lies not in its immediate outcome — Marbury was unsuccessful — but in the detail of the judgement. Though Chief Justice John Marshall admonished Madison, he ruled that the very law under which Marbury brought his case (the Federal Judiciary Act of 1789) violated the US *Constitution*. In his ruling, Marshall also asserted that it was 'emphatically the power and duty of the judicial department to say what the law is'. In accepting the decision in its favour, therefore, Jefferson's administration accepted the right of the Court to void *unconstitutional* statute, thereby establishing the right of *judicial review* over federal law.

Maryland: the seventh state; joined the *Union* in 1788.

Massachusetts: the sixth state; joined the *Union* in 1788.

McCain, John (1936–): a US Senator (Republican–Arizona) and failed candidate for the Republican nomination in the 2000 presidential election. An early favourite in the *media* for the 2008 Republican nomination.

● McCain won the *New Hampshire primary* in 2000 but ultimately lost the Republican nomination race to *George W. Bush*.

● McCain was one of the five Senators caught up in the Keating savings and loans scandal (see *Keating Five*). He was later the joint-sponsor of the *Senate* version of a bill that ultimately became the *Bipartisan Campaign Finance Reform Act (2002)*.

McCarthy, Joseph ('Joe') (1908–57): a US Senator (Republican–Wisconsin) who served between 1947 and 1957, McCarthy's name became synonymous with the anti-Communist witch-hunts common in the USA in the 1950s.

- He first made his name when announcing at a rally in West Virginia that he had in his a hand a list of 205 known Communists working in the State Department.
- McCarthy later became the chair of the Senate Permanent Sub-committee on Investigations. This body held a series of controversial hearings and performed a role similar to the House Un-American Activities Committee (HUAC) in the *House of Representatives.*
- McCarthy's increasingly outrageous and largely unsubstantiated claims led ultimately to his censure by the *Senate* in 1954 for behaviour 'contrary to senatorial traditions'.
- The adjective 'McCarthyite' is now commonly applied to any witch-hunt of the type orchestrated by McCarthy or those individuals that engage in such activity.

McConnell v Federal Election Commission (2003): a case in which the US *Supreme Court* upheld the major provisions of the 2002 *Bipartisan Campaign Finance Reform Act (BCRA).*

McCorvey, Norma (1947–): better known by her pseudonym, Jane Roe, McCorvey was the women at the heart of the landmark US *Supreme Court* case *Roe* v *Wade* (1973).

- Victory in the case came too late for McCorvey who took the pregnancy to term, giving birth to a daughter.
- Despite her involvement in landmark *pro-choice* case, McCorvey later became an active supporter of the *pro-life* movement and a convert to Roman Catholicism.
- **e.g.** In 2005 she petitioned the US Supreme Court, unsuccessfully, to have the *Roe* ruling overturned.

McGovern-Fraser Commission: established at the 1968 Democratic National Convention, a body established to investigate ways in which participation in the presidential nomination could be extended.

- Up to 1968, the process by which delegates were chosen to attend the Convention was dominated by party insiders and *caucuses.*
- Only 11.7 million voters (11% of the voting age population) were involved in the primary phase of the 1968 presidential election.
- The candidate chosen by the *Democratic Party* at the 1968 Convention, *Hubert Humphrey*, had only secured 2.2% of the vote across all *primaries.* Eugene McCarthy had 38.0% and *Robert Kennedy*, who was assassinated after the California primary, won 30.6%.
- The Commission's recommendations were largely responsible for the more widespread use of primary elections from 1972.

▦ **e.g.** By 1988, 20 years after the Commission was established, 35 million Americans (21% of the voting age population) were involved in the nomination process.

▦ **TIP** Although the Commission was established by the Democrats, the spread of primary elections was largely brought about as a result of the subsequent changes made to many states' electoral regulations. As a result, the *Republican Party*'s nomination process in many states was changed also.

McGovern, George (1922–): a former *Democratic Party* member of the US *House of Representatives* and *Senate*. He is best remembered for his landslide defeat to Republican incumbent *Richard Nixon* in the 1972 presidential election.

McKinley, William (1843–1901): the twenty fifth US *president*, 1897–1901.

media: refers to a range of mass communications that include the broadcast media (e.g. television, radio), the press (e.g. newspapers, journals, magazines), and new media (e.g. the internet).

● Although newspapers such as the *New York Times* and the *Washington Post* are available across the USA, the vast majority of US papers are state-wide or local.

● The internet has come to the fore in recent years, e.g. in 2004, blogs and internet chat-rooms spread rumours suggesting that George Bush had been fed lines through an earpiece during the first televised presidential debate.

● In the USA candidates can produce and broadcast as many ads as they can afford to. Paid media is, however, very expensive. A typical 30-second local television ad can cost up to $1,000 and the total amount of money spent on ads increased by 400% to $1 billion between 1982 and 2002, according to the *Washington Times*.

● In 30-second slots candidates often find it easier to make a negative attack on their opponent than offer anything positive in their own favour.

▦ **e.g.** George Bush's 1988 'Willie Horton' ad targeted Democrat *Michael Dukakis*'s record on prisoner release whilst governor of Massachusetts.

▦ **COMPARATIVE** Whereas UK terrestrial television broadcasters are legally required to remain politically impartial, newspapers are free to take sides. The *Sun* was famously vocal in support of the Conservatives in the 1992 general election, coming up with such memorable headlines as 'Will the last person to leave Britain please turn out the light' when a Labour victory appeared likely.

▦ **TIP** The rise of the media has resulted in the more charismatic and telegenic candidates coming to the fore in a politics where the 'sound-bite' conquers all.

media theory: refers to the various models established in order to explain the various levels of interaction between the *media*, individuals within society, and society as a whole.

● See *hegemonic theory, manipulative theory* and *pluralist theory*.

MEDICAID: established under the Social Security Act of 1965 and administered by individual US states, a programme designed to provide health insurance for those on low incomes.

- The federal government establishes service requirements and monitors state provision.

MEDICARE: established alongside MEDICAID in 1965 and administered by the US government, a health insurance programme covering those who are age 65 years or older.

▓ *COMPARATIVE* In the UK, the establishment of a welfare state that would provide a wide range of health and other social services 'from the cradle to the grave' was established in the wake of the Second World War by the Labour government led by Prime Minister Clement Attlee.

Metro Broadcasting Inc. **v** *Federal Communications Commission* **(1990):** a case in which the US *Supreme Court* ruled that a Federal Communications Commission *affirmative action* programme favouring minority broadcasters was allowable under the US *Constitution*.

Michels' iron law of oligarchy: first advanced by German sociologist Robert Michels in 1911, the theory that popular mass movements cannot remain truly democratic because, regardless of their beginnings, they will always end up being controlled by a small guiding elite (an oligarchy).

Michigan: the twenty-sixth state; joined the *Union* in 1837.

Michigan **v** *Tucker* **(1974):** a case in which the US *Supreme Court* ruled that the 'Miranda warnings' were not in themselves rights protected by the US *Constitution*. See *Miranda* v *Arizona (1966)* and *Duckworth* v *Eagan (1989)*.

mid-term elections: the elections for the *House of Representatives* and around one-third of the *Senate* that take place on the first Tuesday after the first Monday in November, mid-way between consecutive presidential elections.

▓ *e.g.* the mid-term elections of 2006 where the *Democratic Party* took control of both the House of Representatives and the Senate.

▓ *TIP* The 2006 mid-term elections also saw the election of 36 of the 50 state governors.

Midwest: refers to the central-northern US states. The term has been in common usage since the nineteenth century.

- The Midwest covers a contiguous region of 12 states including Iowa, Kansas, Nebraska and Ohio.

Million Mom March: part of a campaign for meaningful and sensible gun laws, a march on Washington DC that took place on Mother's Day in 2000 and was said to involve between 600,000 and 800,000 individuals.

- Marches and meetings held in sympathy around the USA were said to have taken place and the total involved over the 1,000,000 mark.

▓ *TIP* The march is a good example of the use of more traditional forms of protest in the USA.

Mills, Charles Wright (1916–62): an American sociologist best known for his book *The Power Elite*. See *elites theory*.

Mineta, Norman (1931–): US secretary for transportation between 2001 and July 2006, Mineta is widely regarded as one of the most successful Asian-American politicians in US history.

● Mineta is unusual in that he was the only Democrat to serve in Republican *George W. Bush*'s first cabinet.

Minnesota: the thirty-second state; joined the *Union* in 1858.

minor parties: see *third parties*.

Miranda v Arizona (1966): a landmark case in which the US *Supreme Court* ruled that criminal suspects had to be informed of their rights prior to questioning by the police.

● The Court's decision was rooted in the *Fifth Amendment*'s protection against self-incrimination (the right to silence).

● The Miranda case resulted in the police carrying cards printed with a carefully worded warning that could be read to suspects at the time of arrest as a way of informing them of their Fifth Amendment rights. This was known as the 'Miranda warning'.

▨ *e.g.* The Miranda warning included four key reminders: first, that there was a right to remain silent; second, that anything that was said by the suspect could be used in evidence against him; third, that the accused had a right to an attorney; and fourth, that one would be provided free of charge if the suspect could not afford to employ one.

▨ *TIP* Initially evidence taken without the Miranda warning having been read could not be used. Later, in cases such as *Duckworth v Eagan (1989)*, the Supreme Court ruled that the exact wording of the Miranda warning did not have to be used in order for any subsequent confession to be valid.

Mississippi: the twentieth state; joined the *Union* in 1817.

Missouri: the twenty-fourth state; joined the *Union* in 1821.

mobocracy: believed by some to be the inevitable consequence of pure democracy, a form of government where decisions are made simply in response to the demands of the majority, rather than by recourse to reason or to the judgement of those elected to govern.

● Commonly said to be a synonym for the word 'ochlocracy', from the Greek *okhlokratia*; 'okhlos' meaning 'mob' and 'kratia' meaning 'power'.

● The *Founding Fathers*' supposed fear of mobocracy was said to have resulted in the inclusion of a number of checking devices in the constitutional settlement agreed at Philadelphia in 1787.

▨ *e.g.* The institution of staggered elections for the *House*, the *Senate* and the *president* was designed to prevent a party with mass support from gaining control of the entire political system in a single electoral event. The establishment of the *Electoral College* is also said to be evidence of the Founding Fathers' fear of unfettered popular democracy.

Mondale, Walter (1928–): former US Senator (Democrat), *vice-president* to *Jimmy Carter* (1977–81) and failed *Democratic Party* presidential candidate in 1984.

- Republican incumbent *Ronald Reagan*'s landslide victory over Mondale in the 1984 presidential election was one of the most comprehensive on record. Mondale only won in his home state of Minnesota and in Washington DC.

Monicagate: see *Monica Lewinsky*.

Monroe, James (1758–1831): the fifth US *president*, 1817–25.

- A close ally of *Thomas Jefferson*, Monroe was best known for issuing what is known as the 'Monroe Doctrine', which set out US opposition to European expansion anywhere in the Americas.

Montana: the forty-first state; joined the *Union* in 1889.

Montesquieu, Baron de (1689–1755): Charles Louis de Secondat Montesquieu, Baron de la Brède, was a French philosopher whose ideas greatly influenced the *Founding Fathers*.

- Montesquieu is best remembered for writing *The Spirit of the Laws* (1748). This philosophical work, in 31 volumes, addressed a broad range of political, social and legal matters. Most significantly, it advanced the doctrine of the *separation of powers*.
- This doctrine was a major consideration for those framing the US *Constitution* in 1787

Moral Majority: an evangelical Christian lobby group founded in 1979 by tele-vangelist *Jerry Falwell* and a small group of individuals who had left an earlier group, Christian Voice, following a split.

- The group was an umbrella for the numerous Christian political action committees that existed in the USA at the time.
- The Moral Majority was formally disbanded in 1989, though groups such as the Rev. Pat Robertson's Christian Coalition carried on its work.
- **e.g.** The Moral Majority claimed to have registered around 10 million new voters for *Ronald Reagan* between 1979 and 1984.

motor voter law: shorthand for the *National Voter Registration Act* (NVRA), signed into law by President *Bill Clinton* in 1993.

- The Act aimed to improve levels of *voter registration* by requiring state governments to make the registration process easier.
- **e.g.** The Act became know as the motor voter law because it allowed citizens to register to vote at the same time as they completed their driver licence registration.
- **TIP** See *voter registration drives*.
- **COMPARATIVE** The importance of voter registration in the USA stems from the fact that it is not compulsory. As a result, some groups (e.g. Hispanics and black Americans) register at far lower levels than the population taken as a whole. This means that large numbers of potential Hispanic and black voters are effectively disenfranchised at election time. In the UK, voter registration is less of an issue as a result of the fact that it is a legal requirement.

NAACP: see *National Association for the Advancement of Colored People*.

Nader, Ralph (1934–): a consumer rights champion and unsuccessful Green Party candidate in the 2000 presidential election in which he secured 2.9% of the vote (over 3 million votes) nationally. Nader also ran as an independent presidential candidate in 2004.

- Many credit Nader's consumer activism with a number of major developments including the creation of the *Environmental Protection Agency* and the introduction of compulsory seat-belts in cars in the USA.
- In the 2000 presidential election Nader secured 87,974 votes in the key *swing-state* of Florida, before any of the recounts had started. At that point, *George W. Bush*'s margin of victory over *Al Gore* in Florida was only 1,784 votes.

■ *TIP* Nader was accused of splitting the 'anti-Bush vote' in 2000 and thereby allowing the election of a president (i.e. George W. Bush) who was likely to be far worse for the environment than the man who would have won had Nader not stood for election, the then Democratic candidate, later environmental campaigner Al Gore.

NAFTA: see *North American Free Trade Association*.

NARAL: see *National Abortion Rights Action League*.

NASA: see *National Aeronautics and Space Administration*.

National Abortion Rights Action League (NARAL): a *pro-choice pressure group* active in the USA since its creation in 1969.

- The group was known as the National Association for the Repeal of Abortion Laws before the *Roe* v *Wade* case of 1973.
- NARAL campaigns to remove existing restrictions on *abortion* and move towards a situation where the procedure is available on demand.

National Aeronautics and Space Administration (NASA): established in 1958, NASA is the federal government agency responsible for the US space programme. It also has a responsibility for aerospace research in general.

National Association for the Advancement of Colored People (NAACP): founded in 1909, an influential civil rights organisation that works on behalf of ethnic minority groups, most notably black Americans.

- The group was especially active in the 1950s and 1960s.

e.g. The NAACP provided legal support for the plaintiffs in the landmark *Brown v Board of Education* case of 1954.

National Industrial Recovery Act (NIRA) (1933): part of the *New Deal* programme of *Franklin D. Roosevelt*, the NIRA gave the *president* wide-ranging powers to regulate business and create jobs for those who were unemployed as a result of the *Great Depression*.

● The Act also established the National Recovery Administration, an *executive agency*.

National Organization for Women (NOW): founded in 1966, a US *pressure group* that campaigns to end discrimination on the basis of gender.

● NOW had more than half a million members in 2007.

e.g. The group campaigned in favour of the *Equal Rights Amendment* in the 1970s and 1980s and was also active in its opposition to the confirmation of *Supreme Court* Justice *Clarence Thomas* in 1991. During his *Senate* confirmation hearings Thomas had been accused of sexual harassment by a former colleague, Anita Hill.

National Rifle Association (NRA): originally founded as the American Rifle Association in 1871, a US *pressure group* that campaigns to protect the right to bear arms *entrenched* in the *Second Amendment* to the US *Constitution*.

● The NRA had around 4.5 million members in 2007.

● The group is active in providing campaign finance for candidates who are in sympathy with its aims.

e.g. In the year that ended with the 2000 presidential election the NRA's *political action committee* was ranked first in terms of receipts (i.e. monies raised) by the *Federal Election Commission*, with receipts of $17,881,886.

TIP See *gun control*.

national security advisor (NSA): the chief advisor to the *president* on issues relating to national security. The NSA is a leading figure on the *National Security Council* (NSC).

e.g. *Condoleezza Rice* was NSA in *George W. Bush*'s first term, before taking on the role of secretary of state in the wake of his re-election in 2004.

TIP Historically there has often been tension between the NSA and the secretary of state. Under *Jimmy Carter*, for example, there were problems between Zbigniew Brzezinski (NSA) and Secretary of State Cyrus Vance. There was also said to be tension between *Colin Powell* (secretary of state) and Rice (NSA) in *George W. Bush*'s first term. See also *Henry Kissinger*.

National Security Council (NSC): created in 1947 by the National Security Act, the NSC has the role of coordinating policy relating to national security, both domestic and foreign.

● The NSC is headed by the *national security advisor* (NSA) and includes the *president*, the *vice-president*, and the secretaries of state and defense, with occasional visits from the CIA head and the chiefs of staff.

- *Henry Kissinger* was a key figure in expanding the role of the NSC under *Richard Nixon*. Kissinger kept the title of national security advisor even when he became the secretary of state.

National Voter Registration Act (1993): see *motor voter law*.

Nebraska: the thirty-seventh state; joined the *Union* in 1867.

■ *TIP* The state is unusual in that it has a unicameral *legislature*. Nebraska is also notable for the fact that it awards its *Electoral College* votes under the *Maine System*.

necessary and proper clause (or 'elastic clause'): the final clause in Article 1, section 8 of the US *Constitution*.

- The clause states that *Congress* shall have power 'To make all laws which shall be necessary and proper for carrying into Execution the foregoing Powers, and all other Powers vested by this Constitution in the Government of the United States, or in any Department of Officer thereof'.

■ *e.g.* The clause has been used to provide legal justification for much of the expansion in federal government activity that has taken place since the 1930s.

■ *TIP* Commonly known as the 'elastic clause' as it is regarded as a 'catch-all' or 'blank cheque' that affords Congress the power to do what needs to be done. In reality, the use of the clause has been closely monitored by the US *Supreme Court*.

negative campaigning: a style of electioneering that focuses on the perceived or imagined weaknesses of an opponent rather than advancing a positive agenda of one's own.

- Such campaigning may focus on an opponent's policies or on their character.

■ *e.g.* See *attack ads* and *Willie Horton ad*.

negative rights: see *positive rights*.

Neustadt, Richard (1919–2003): an American historian and political scientist best known for his book *Presidential Power*, first published in 1960.

- Neustadt's ideas were informed by his experience as an advisor to several presidents including *Harry Truman*.

- He recognised that the *Constitution* had established a system of 'separated institutions sharing powers', as opposed to a full *separation of powers*.

- The fluidity in the relationship between the *executive* and the *legislature* in particular allowed capable presidents to extend the scope and extent of their power. As a result, the power of the president was, Neustadt maintained, 'the power to persuade'.

Nevada: the thirty-sixth state; joined the *Union* in 1864.

New Deal: a series of government programmes and initiatives introduced by President *Franklin D. Roosevelt* in response to the *Great Depression*.

■ *e.g.* See *Agricultural Adjustment Act* and *National Industrial Recovery Act*.

New Democrats: an organised centre-right faction within the *Democratic Party* that is associated with the Democratic Leadership Council (DLC).

- The defeat of more traditional 'liberal' Democratic presidential candidates in 1968 (*Humphrey*), 1972 (*McGovern*), 1984 (*Mondale*), and 1988 (*Dukakis*) led many Democrats to conclude that the party had to broaden its appeal.
- The party's only success during this period was the victory of *Jimmy Carter* in 1976, a southern Democrat running against a *Republican Party* tainted by the *Watergate Scandal*.
- The DLC looked to move the party to the right.
- **e.g.** New Democrat *Bill Clinton* was the first Democrat since *Franklin D. Roosevelt* to serve two terms as president. He accepted a broadly neo-liberal approach in economics, famously announcing that the era of big government was over.
- **COMPARATIVE** Comparisons are often drawn between the rise of the New Democrats in the USA and the emergence of New Labour in the UK.

new federalism: an approach characterised by the return of certain powers and responsibilities from the federal government to the governments of the various US states.

- It is often seen as an attempt to reverse the growth in central government interventionism that had begun with *Franklin D. Roosevelt*'s *New Deal*.
- New federalism is closely associated with the *Reagan* administrations of the 1980s and his contention that government was 'part of the problem' rather than 'part of the solution'.
- **e.g.** Republican domination of the White House in the period 1970–93 led to plans to reduce federal grants as part of the budget-balancing programme. The *Supreme Court* also took the lead by, for example, allowing states to limit access to *abortion* by passing laws that appeared to undermine the 1973 *Roe* v *Wade* ruling, e.g. *Webster* v *Reproductive Health Services (1989).*
- **TIP** Those looking to return powers to the states argued that the *Tenth Amendment*'s guarantee of states' rights (the *reserved powers*) had been ignored since the 1930s.

New Frontier: originally a phrase used by *John F. Kennedy* in a speech accepting the Democratic nomination for the 1960 presidential election, the phrase was later applied to Kennedy's domestic and foreign policy agenda whilst in office.

- Though much of what Kennedy tried to do was cut short by his assassination in 1963, some of the New Frontier initiatives were later realised in *Lyndon Johnson*'s *Great Society* programme.
- **e.g.** Kennedy's advocacy of civil rights paved the way for Johnson's *Civil Rights Act (1964).*

New Hampshire: the ninth state; joined the *Union* in 1788.

New Hampshire primary: by tradition the first primary contest in each presidential election year. It is seen as a key early testing ground for the candidates seeking each party's nomination.

- Although New Hampshire is a small and unrepresentative state it provides an early focus for *media* coverage.

- Success in this early test allows a candidate to build up campaign momentum (the 'Big Mo'). This is partly due to the fact that candidates who win in New Hampshire, and the Iowa *caucus* that precedes it, often attract new financial backers. See *front-loading.*
- Although victory in this primary was once seen as essential for any candidate wishing to win his/her party's nomination, recent years have witnessed a number of candidates who have lost New Hampshire yet still recovered to represent their party in the November election.
- ▥ *e.g. Bill Clinton* for the Democrats (1992) and *George W. Bush* for the Republicans (2000) both lost the New Hampshire primary but were ultimately successful in securing their party's nomination, and in winning the presidential election that followed.

New Jersey: the third state; joined the *Union* in 1787.

New Jersey Plan (1787): a response to the *Virginia Plan* advanced by the more populous states, the New Jersey Plan argued that each state should be represented equally in the new US *legislature,* regardless of population.

- Under the *Connecticut Compromise* this idea of equal representation was later adopted for the US *Senate* (with two Senators per state).

New Mexico: the forty-seventh state; joined the *Union* in 1912.

New Right: a wide-ranging political movement that combined the traditional conservative policies of laissez-faire economics and social conservatism with a greater willingness to get involved on the international stage.

- The New Right had strong links with the evangelical Christian movement in the USA. As a result they opposed *abortion,* homosexuality, and pornography.
- ▥ *e.g.* The election of *Ronald Reagan* as president in 1980 was widely seen as a triumph for the New Right.
- ▥ *COMPARATIVE* In the UK, the influence of the New Right agenda can be seen in the neo-liberalism and Thatcherism of the 1980s onwards.

New York: the eleventh state; joined the *Union* in 1788.

***New York Times* v *United States* (1971):** a case in which the US *Supreme Court* ruled that President *Richard Nixon* did not have the power to prevent the *New York Times* and the *Washington Post* publishing *Pentagon* papers that the *executive* had classified as secret.

- The Court decided that the right to publish the material (protected by the *First Amendment'*s guarantee of a free press) outweighed any power that the executive might have to classify information on the basis of the powers afforded the president in Article 2 of the US *Constitution.*

***New York* v *Quarles* (1984):** a case in which the US *Supreme Court* recognised a 'public safety exemption' to the guidelines it established in the 1966 *Miranda* v *Arizona* case.

9/11: shorthand for the coordinated terrorist attacks against major US targets that occurred on 11 September 2001.

- Al Qaeda terrorists planned to destroy the World Trade Center, the *Pentagon* and the White House by flying hi-jacked commercial airliners into their targets.
- The iconic Twin Towers of the World Trade Center were entirely destroyed with the lost of nearly 3,000 lives. The Pentagon building, housing the *Defense Department*, was badly damaged. Another aircraft crashed in Pennsylvania en route to its supposed target, the White House, possibly as a result of the efforts of passengers seeking to overpower the hijackers.
- The attacks were used as justification for *George W. Bush*'s *War on Terror* and the invasions of Afghanistan and Iraq that followed.
- **TIP** Some argue that 9/11 allowed the Bush administration to bring in measures that restricted personal liberties (see *Patriot Act* and *Guantanamo Bay*).

Nineteenth Amendment (1920): guaranteed the right to vote regardless of sex (i.e. gender).

- Though many US states had already extended the right to vote to women as well as men by 1920, this amendment applied the rule nationwide.

Ninth Amendment (1791): confirmed that US citizens retain rights that are not explicitly set out in the US *Constitution*.

- Some states already had laws that provided a greater degree of protection than that afforded by one or more elements of the proposed *Bill of Rights*. Many believed in the notion of inalienable natural rights.
- They feared that the enumeration of certain liberties in the US Bill of Rights would give the impression that any freedoms omitted had been lost or were of lower status. The Ninth Amendment addressed these fears.
- **COMPARATIVE** The question of what to include and what to leave out when framing a bill of rights has also presented a problem to advocates of a formal UK Bill of Rights.

NIRA: see *National Industrial Recovery Act*.

Nixon, Richard M. (1913–94): the thirty-seventh US *president*, serving between 1969 and his resignation in 1974. He was previously a *vice-president* to *Dwight Eisenhower* (1953–61) and failed Republican candidate in the 1960 presidential election, where he lost to *John F. Kennedy*.

- Nixon's time in office is most often remembered for the events surrounding the *Watergate Scandal* that precipitated his resignation in 1974. See also *United States* v *Richard Nixon (1974)*.
- The period also saw momentous developments in foreign policy, e.g. the US withdrawal from Vietnam and the opening of diplomatic relations with China.

No Child Left Behind Act (NCLB) (2001): a US law that authorised a number of federal government programmes designed to improve the performance and *accountability* of US primary and secondary schools.

- The NCLB placed a greater emphasis on improving levels of literacy.
- It also offered greater parent choice in respect of the allocation of school places.

nomination process: a mechanism by which an individual is selected as a party's official candidate in an election.

● See *caucuses, primaries,* and *party conventions.*

North American Free Trade Agreement (NAFTA): an agreement between the USA, Canada and Mexico that created the North American Free Trade Area.

● NAFTA was widely seen as an attempt to counter the growing size and economic power of the EU.

● The plan involved the gradual removal of the majority of tariffs that had operated on trade between the three nations.

● *Bill Clinton's vice-president, Al Gore,* was widely credited with pushing through the negotiations that saw NAFTA established.

■ *TIP* Opposition to NAFTA was a key plank of *Ross Perot's Reform Party* candidacy in the 1992 presidential election. Perot predicted that the conclusion of any deal would be immediately followed by a giant 'sucking sound'; the sound, he said, of US jobs being sucked into Mexico.

North Carolina: the twelfth state; joined the *Union* in 1789.

North Dakota: the thirty-ninth state; joined the *Union* in 1889.

Norton, Gale (1954–): US secretary of the interior under *George W. Bush* between 2001 and 2006. The first woman to hold the post since the department was established in 1849.

NOW: see *National Organization of Women.*

NRA: see *National Rifle Association.*

NSA: see *national security advisor.*

NSC: see *National Security Council.*

Obama, Barack (1961–): a *Democratic Party* politician and the only *African-American* US Senator at the time that he was elected to represent the state of Illinois in 2004.

- Obama's 2004 senatorial campaign was memorable for the well-received key-note speech he gave at the Democratic National Convention.
- In February 2007 Obama announced his intention to seek his party's nomination in the 2008 presidential election.

O'Connor, Sandra Day (1930–): the first woman to serve on the US *Supreme Court*, O'Connor was appointed by *Ronald Reagan* in 1981. She retired in 2006 and was replaced on the Court by *Samuel Alito*.

- Though O'Connor was appointed by a Republican president, she was regarded as the 'swing vote' for much of her last decade on the Court.

■ *e.g.* O'Connor's unwillingness to see the *precedent* established under the 1973 *Roe* v *Wade* ruling overturned led her to side with the more liberal justices on the Court in a number of cases relating to the issue of *abortion*.

■ *TIP* Many felt that replacing O'Connor (the 'swing vote') with a committed conservative Justice such as Alito would fundamentally shift the balance of the Court to the right.

Office of Management and Budget (OMB): employing around 500 professional staff, the OMB is one of the largest and most important bodies within the *Executive Office of the President (EXOP)*. It plays a central role in researching and putting together the president's annual budget request to *Congress*.

- The Office provides advice to the president's team on a wide range of management and budgetary issues and also plays a role in ensuring smooth coordination across the *executive*.
- The OMB has to put together a budget request that will balance the needs of the various *executive departments*, agencies, regulatory commissions, and other bodies.
- The importance of the OMB is underlined by the fact that the president needs *Senate* confirmation for his appointments to six positions within the Office. These include the posts of director and deputy director.

■ *e.g.* In January 2007 the director of the OMB was Rob Portman.

O

Ohio: the seventeenth state; joined the *Union* in 1803.

● Ohio was one of the crucial *swing states* in the 2004 presidential election.

***Ohio v Akron Center for Reproductive Health Inc.* (1990):** a case in which the US *Supreme Court* ruled that parents of minors seeking abortions should be informed before the procedure could take place.

▉ *TIP* This case is a good example of the way in which the US Supreme Court has looked to clarify its view on the availability of *abortion* without going as far as to overturn the precedent set by *Roe* v *Wade* (1973).

Oklahoma: the forty-sixth state; joined the *Union* in 1907.

Oklahoma City bombing (19 April 1995): an attack on a federal government building for which Timothy McVeigh was convicted and later executed by lethal injection in 2001.

● McVeigh and two other conspirators were angry at what they saw as the heavy-handed way in which a number of federal law enforcement agencies — specifically the Federal Bureau of Investigations (FBI) and the Bureau of Alcohol, Tobacco and Firearms (ATF) — had dealt with the incidents at *Waco* and *Ruby Ridge*.

● Their attack was designed to be part of a broader campaign against what they saw as federal government interference in the everyday lives of law-abiding US citizens.

● The attack, which initial press reports speculated might be the work of al Qaeda, destroyed the Alfred P. Murrah building, killing 168 and injuring a further 800.

OMB: see *Office of Management and Budget.*

opinion poll: most visible at election times when professional polling companies question the voting intentions of sample groups selected with the aim of re-creating a true cross-section of the *electorate* in a group normally in excess of 1,000 individuals. See *base-line poll, tracking poll,* and *exit poll.*

▉ *COMPARATIVE* In some countries (France for example) opinion polls are banned in the days leading up to elections for fear that they might influence voting intentions. See *bandwagon effect* and *boomerang effect.*

Oregon: the thirty-third state; joined the *Union* in 1859.

oversight: a term referring to the work of *Congress* in overseeing or scrutinising the activities of the *executive.*

● Much of this oversight function is performed within congressional *standing committees.* These committees have the power of subpoena, allowing them to call for documentary evidence and require key officers of the executive to give oral testimony before them.

● Under the Legislative Reorganisation Act of 1947, these committees also have the power to scrutinise government agencies that fall within their area of legislative competence.

● Oversight can also take the form of special investigations involving the formation of ad hoc committees.

▉ *e.g.* the joint committee that investigated the *Iran-Contra affair.*

■ *TIP* Taken in a broader sense the term can refer to the many ways in which the US Congress can check the executive's powers of patronage, its foreign policy powers, or its legislative ambitions.

■ *COMPARATIVE* In the UK, the term 'scrutiny' is often used as a synonym for 'oversight'. Prime Minister's Question Time (PMQT) is an example of Commons scrutiny of the executive.

PAC: see *political action committee*.

Paige, Rod (1933–): the first *African-American* to serve as US secretary of education, Paige was a member of *George W. Bush*'s *cabinet* between 2001 and 2005. His period in office is closely associated with the *No Child Left Behind Act (2001)*.

Paine, Thomas (1737–1809): a British-born radical and pamphleteer best known for his work, *The Rights of Man*.

● Paine was involved in the *American War of Independence* (American Revolution), having emigrated to the colonies. His influential pamphlet, *Common Sense*, set out the case for an independent America.

● His writings were said to be a key influence on the *Founding Fathers* and on those who led the French Revolution.

partial birth abortion: a colloquial term normally referring to the intact dilation and extraction (IDX) method of *abortion*.

● IDX became a focus for the US abortion debate because the procedure involves removing the entire foetus intact, thus providing a powerful visual image for *pro-life* campaigners.

partisan alignment: referring to the degree of correlation that may exist between party identification and voting patterns.

● High levels of partisan alignment would see Democrat identifiers voting consistently for *Democratic Party* candidates.

▓ *e.g.* In the 2004 presidential election 89% of Democrat identifiers voted for *John Kerry* (i.e. Democrat) and 93% of Republican identifiers voted for *George W. Bush* (i.e. Republican).

▓ *COMPARATIVE* In the UK, strong class alignment and strong partisan alignment were commonly advanced as key elements of the 'primacy' and 'social structures' models of *voting behaviour*. A decline in both has accompanied a rise in the importance of 'recency' factors such as candidates, campaigns, issues, and events. See *independent voters*.

party: a group of like-minded individuals who come together in order to seek power — most often by seeking election to office — as a means of achieving their shared goals.

COMPARATIVE In the UK, political parties were once said to represent distinct ideological traditions. In the US, however, political parties have always been decidedly broad churches. As eminent American historian Richard Hofstadter observed, it was America's destiny 'not to have an ideology but to be one'.

party-building activities: events and campaigns designed to build up political parties at a grassroots level.

- In 1979 *Congress* passed an Act that exempted such activities from the campaign finance restrictions imposed under the 1974 *Federal Election Campaign Act (FECA)*.

- As a result, unregulated money (called *soft money*) could be collected and spent on such activities.

e.g. Such FECA-exempt party-building activities included *voter registration drives* and *get out the vote campaigns*.

party convention: the quadrennial conferences organised by both of the main US political parties, and some *third parties* also. These conventions serve the formal roles of selecting each party's presidential and vice-presidential candidates (collectively known as 'the *ticket*'), and agreeing the policies on which they will stand (the *platform*).

- The platform has become less of an issue in recent years as campaigns have become more *candidate-centred* and *media*-driven.

- The rise of *primary elections* and 'committed delegates' has meant that each party's presidential candidate is normally known well before the convention starts.

- It has also become common for prospective presidential candidates to name their *running mates* ahead of the national convention.

e.g. In 2004 both tickets (Kerry–Edwards and Bush–Cheney) were known pre-convention. The same was true in 2000 (Gore–Lieberman and Bush–Cheney).

TIP Although the formal roles of the party conventions have been undermined in recent decades, such events still play a number of important informal roles. In the modern era conventions focus on courting the media and raising campaign finance. Parties aim to show a united front with candidates looking to benefit from a 'post-convention bounce' in the polls if things go well.

party leaders: in the absence of formally elected US party leaders, this term would normally refer to individuals such as the chairs of each party's national committee (see *DNC* and *RNC*) and senior leadership figures within *Congress* (see *majority and minority leaders*, and *whips*).

- The chairs of the *House* and *Senate* campaign committees also take on a genuine leadership role at election time.

e.g. See *Rahm Emanuel*.

party platform: a summary of the positions taken by a political party on a range of issues, most often revised and published ahead of an election.

- Individual platform policies are referred to as 'planks'.

▓ *e.g.* From 1992 the *Democratic Party* had a platform that was *pro-choice* on the issue of *abortion*, whereas the *Republican Party* platform was *pro-life*.

▓ *TIP* Not withstanding their differences on issues such as abortion, US party platforms have traditionally been seen as overly vague. However, in the wake of the Democrats' defeat in the 2004 presidential election *Howard Dean* — the newly elected chair of the *Democratic National Committee* — launched a '50-state strategy' that included a commitment to produce more meaningful and distinctive election platforms.

▓ *COMPARATIVE* In the UK, the term 'manifesto' is used as a synonym for 'platform'.

party system: refers collectively to the major parties within a given country, the relationships between them and the political structures and processes that have brought about and in turn perpetuate this state of affairs.

● The USA is generally said to be a two-party system due to the fact that the Democrats and the Republicans fill virtually every elected office at federal and state level.

▓ *e.g.* In the 110th *Congress*, which met in January 2007, all 435 members of the *House of Representatives* were Democrats or Republicans (233:202).

● *COMPARATIVE* The UK is still generally seen as a two-party system, though the emergence of a stronger third party presence in the Commons and the resurgence of nationalist parties in Scotland and Wales has led some to speak of a multi-party system operating, in some areas at least. Of the 646 MPs elected in 2005, 553 represented Labour or the Conservatives. This equates to 85.6% of the House of Commons.

passage of legislation: the process by which a bill becomes a law.

Patriot Act (2001): formally signed into law by *George W. Bush* in October 2001, the Patriot Act massively expanded the powers of US law enforcement agencies as a means of combating the threat posed by terrorism.

● The Act was introduced in the wake of *9/11*. The immediate reaction to the attacks ensured that the bill was passed with little opposition in either the *House* or the *Senate*.

● The Act was renewed in March 2006.

▓ *TIP* The ease with which the Act passed *Congress* is a good illustration of the extent to which a *president* can force controversial measures through the *legislature* in times of emergency by 'wrapping himself in the flag'.

● *COMPARATIVE* The UK government responded to the attacks of 9/11 by passing the Anti-terrorism, Crime and Security Act (2001), which authorised the indefinite detention of terrorist suspects without trial.

PDB: see *presidential daily briefing*.

peak groups: organisations that coordinate the efforts of a number of groups sharing common interests. Also referred to as 'umbrella groups'.

▓ *e.g.* See *American Federation of Labor–Congress of Industrial Organisations (AFL-CIO)*.

Pendleton Act (1883): a federal Act that established the US Civil Service Commission and replaced the old *spoils system* with a more meritocratic procedure for appointments to most positions in the *federal bureaucracy*.

- The Act was in part a response to the assassination of President *James Garfield* by Charles Julius Guiteau in 1881. Guiteau had acted following Secretary of State James G. Blane's decision not to appoint him as an ambassador.

Pennsylvania: the second state; joined the *Union* in 1787.

Pentagon: the headquarters of the US *Department of Defense* in Arlington, Virginia. Its name refers to the shape of the complex when viewed from the air.

- The Pentagon was one of the hijackers' targets on *9/11*.

penumbra: literally, a partial shadow. In politics the term 'penumbras' is commonly used to refer to the hidden meanings or inferences read into the *Constitution* by the US *Supreme Court* when performing its role of *judicial review*.

- *e.g.* The constitutional protection of privacy — and with it the right to *abortion* — is rooted in the penumbras emanating from the *First, Fourth, Fifth* and *Ninth Amendments*.

Perot, [Henry] Ross (1930–): billionaire founder of the *Reform Party* and its candidate in the 1992 and 1996 presidential elections.

- Perot made his fortune by building up and ultimately selling Electronic Data Systems, a company he founded in the 1960s.

- He ran for the White House in 1992 on a *platform* of balanced budget fiscal conservatism and opposition to the *North American Free Trade Agreement (NAFTA)*. Some of his ideas were later adopted as part of the Republicans' *Contract with America* platform in the 1994 *mid-term elections*.

- *e.g.* Perot secured 19% of the popular vote in 1992 and 9% in 1996, though he failed to secure any *Electoral College* votes on each occasion. Perot took most of his support from Republicans disillusioned with 'business as usual' in Washington DC. Some argue that Perot's candidacy in 1992 resulted in *Bill Clinton*'s victory.

- *TIP* Perot's 1992 campaign was unusual in that his high ratings in the polls resulted in him being invited to take part in the televised presidential debates with *George H. W. Bush* and Bill Clinton.

Philadelphia Convention (1787): the constitutional convention at which the representatives of all of the former colonies except Rhode Island met to revise the *Articles of Confederation*.

- Those attending the Convention are now commonly referred to as the *Founding Fathers*.

- Though they met ostensibly to revise the Articles of Confederation, many of those present (e.g. *James Madison* and *Alexander Hamilton*) were intent on creating an entirely new system of government.

- The Convention agreed the text of the US *Constitution*, which came into force in 1789 having been ratified by the required number of states.

Pierce, Franklin (1804–69): the fourteenth US *president*, 1853–57.

pigeon-holing: normally refers to the work of *standing committees* and their subcommittees in *Congress*, this is a process by which bills are essentially shelved and allowed to die without being formally discussed or reported-out to the floor of the legislative chamber.

- The power to prioritise bills within committee, and thereby pigeon-hole those they deem less worthy of consideration, has traditionally been wielded by committee chairmen.

***Planned Parenthood of South-eastern Pennsylvania* v *Casey* (1992):** a case in which the US *Supreme Court* upheld the constitutionality of a Pennsylvania state law that required a married woman to inform her husband prior to seeking an *abortion*.

- The law in question also imposed mandatory counselling and a 24-hour cooling-off period between the end of this counselling and the procedure itself.

▨ *TIP* This case was seen as a further narrowing of the 1973 *Roe* v *Wade* ruling.

platform: see *party platform*.

***Plessy* v *Ferguson* (1896):** a case in which the US *Supreme Court* ruled that segregation by race was constitutionally allowed under the *Fourteenth Amendment* to the US *Constitution*, providing that the accommodation provided was 'equal'.

- This 'separate but equal' interpretation of the Fourteenth Amendment's equal protection clause provided a legal *precedent* for other forms of segregation. It was invalidated in the landmark 1954 *Brown* v *Board of Education* case.

▨ *TIP* The difference between the Court's rulings in *Plessy* v *Fergusson (1896)* and *Brown* v *Board of Education of Topeka (1954)* provides an excellent example of the quasi-legislative powers available to the Court when interpreting the US Constitution. As the then governor of South Carolina and former Supreme Court Associate Justice James F. Byrnes remarked upon hearing the outcome of the *Brown* case, 'the Court did not interpret the Constitution — the Court amended it'.

pluralism (pluralist democracy): the principle that different groups and interests can exist and compete freely and fairly within a democratic society.

- The principle of pluralism is often said to be particularly relevant to the USA. This is a result of the diversity of American society and the constitutional fragmentation of power brought about by the federal division of power and also by the existence of a *separation of powers* within the federal government.

- Such a fragmentation of power provides numerous access points where groups can exert influence.

- The defining characteristics of US *political culture* are also said to favour democratic pluralism.

▨ *TIP* This pluralist model is undermined by the presence of the kinds of large, wealthy, or high status groups who often come to dominate political decision-making in the USA. See *elites theory*.

- **COMPARATIVE** The UK's traditional status as a unitary state and the fusion of powers that exists between the *executive* and the *legislature* limits the kind of free and fair competition that is synonymous with democratic pluralism.

pluralist theory: the theories associated with the principle of *pluralism*. See above.

pocket veto: see *veto*.

political action committee (PAC): a group that seeks to bring about the election or defeat of specific candidates for political office, most often by providing campaign contributions.

- PACs proliferated in the wake of the *Federal Election Campaign Act (FECA, 1974)*. By placing a $1,000 limit on individual contributions the Act forced individuals to organise PACs. Under the Act, such groups could contribute up to $5,000 per candidate, per election.
- PACs are often portrayed either as the 'financial arm' of *pressure groups*, or as the 'middle-men' who link pressure groups and candidates.
- **e.g.** According to the *Federal Election Commission* there were nearly 5,000 PACs at the time of the 2004 presidential election.
- **TIP** Although the amount of money that an individual PAC can give a candidate is limited under FECA, there is no limit to the number of PACs that can support a single candidate. As a result, PACs favouring candidates with a similar outlook will 'bundle' their contributions.

political culture: the collective values, attitudes and beliefs that influence political behaviour within a nation.

- A nation's political culture shapes the way in which citizens view the state: the extent to which they participate in its processes and accept its *authority*.
- **e.g.** US political culture is traditionally said to be based upon a belief in liberty and *limited government, individualism*, and the *American Dream*.
- **TIP** Generalised discussion of the political culture of any nation as large and diverse as the USA is likely to be undermined by differences at regional, state and local level.
- **COMPARATIVE** UK political culture was traditionally said to be characterised by homogeneity, consensus and deference. Some argue that such principles have been undermined since the 1950s.

Polk, James Knox (1795–1849): the eleventh US *president*, 1845–49.

poll tax: any tax identified as a requirement for a citizen to qualify for the franchise.

- Poll taxes were common in some southern states between the mid-nineteenth century and the 1950s. They proliferated as a de facto means of disenfranchising black voters following the ban on explicit discrimination in voting *entrenched* in the *Fifteenth Amendment* (1870).
- Such taxes also had the effect of disenfranchising many poor white citizens.
- The *Twenty-Fourth Amendment* (1964) explicitly outlawed poll taxes.
- See also *Grandfather Clause*.

■ **COMPARATIVE** In the UK, 'the Poll Tax' is a colloquial name for 'the Community Charge', a form of individual local taxation introduced in 1990 (1989 in Scotland) as a replacement for the property-based rates system. The charge earned its nick-name as a result of the fact that it was payable by all citizens aged 18 or over, those also eligible to vote. Though non-payment of the charge could and often did result in prosecution, it did not disenfranchise the offender. As a result the application of the term was both pejorative and somewhat misleading.

polling: see *opinion poll*.

***Pollock* v *Farmers' Loan and Trust Company* (1895):** a case in which the US *Supreme Court* ruled that federal income tax was *unconstitutional*.

● *Congress* later overturned this precedent by initiating and securing the *ratification* of the *Sixteenth Amendment* (1913), which provided that 'Congress shall have the power to lay and collect taxes on incomes'.

popular sovereignty: a concept based upon the ideas of writers such as *John Locke* and *Jean-Jacques Rousseau*. The view that as the state is, in theory, created by the people, its power depends upon them. As a result, the people have the right to remove any government that goes against the common good.

pork-barrelled bill: a bill weighed down with amendments (known as 'riders') that brings benefits to the *districts* or states of those individual *Congressmen* who added them, yet — in most cases at least — have little to do with the bill's original purpose. Appropriations bills are most often targeted in this way.

● The term 'pork' refers to the federal government contracts, subsidies or other benefits that a Congressman might look to gain for his or her district or state. Congressmen who are successful in such an enterprise are said to be 'bringing home the bacon' or 'taking care of the folks back home'.

■ *e.g.* On 16 April 1986 the *House of Representatives* had to reconsider a bill that was designed to provide aid to the 'Contras' fighting against the Communist Sandinistas in Nicaragua. The *House Rules Committee* supported the bill, but added a 'rider' worth $1.7 billion of supplementary spending for Congressmen's pet projects. This was 170 times the value of the aid that the bill provided to the Contras. *Reagan*'s *aides* described the rider as a 'rancid barrel of pork', a 'shabby and shameful trick'. See *Iran-Contra affair*.

positive rights: commonly refers to those rights explicitly assigned to citizens.

● Often contrasted with negative rights; those freedoms that are not explicitly set out but exist, nonetheless, in the absence of any law forbidding individuals from exercising them.

● The USA is often said to have a 'rights culture' that is rooted in the way in which individual liberties are explicitly *entrenched* in the *Constitution,* e.g. in the US *Bill of Rights* (1791) and in the *Thirteenth* (1865), *Fourteenth* (1865) and *Fifteenth Amendments* (1870).

● Federal laws also play a part in defining the rights available to US citizens.

■ *e.g.* the 1966 *Freedom of Information Act (FOIA)*.

■ *COMPARATIVE* The UK constitution has evolved over time with citizens remaining free to do anything that has not been legislated against. Some argue that this culture of negative rights has been altered as a result of the passage of the Human Rights Act (HRA, 1998) and the Freedom of Information Act (FOIA, 2000).

Powell, Colin (1937–): *national security advisor* under *Ronald Reagan* (1987–89), chairman of the joint chiefs of staff under *George H. W. Bush* (1989–93), and later secretary of state in *George W. Bush*'s first term (2001–05). He was the highest ranking *African-American* serving in the *executive* during his time at the *State Department*.

● In respect of foreign policy, Powell was widely seen as a 'dove' who clashed with 'hawks' such as *Donald Rumsfeld* over policy in Afghanistan and Iraq.

power: the ability to do something or make something happen.

● Power and *authority* can exist together or independently of one another. See *authority*.

precedent: a prior example or event that is taken as a guide when considering a similar set of circumstances occurring subsequently. The term is often used with reference to the way in which court rulings can establish legal precedent.

■ *e.g.* Although the *Supreme Court*'s 1954 *Brown* v *Board of Education* ruling concerned segregation in schools in Topeka, Kansas, it established the broader precedent that segregation violated the *Fourteenth Amendment*, a precedent that was confined neither to schools, nor to Kansas.

■ *COMPARATIVE* In the UK, legal precedent is more commonly known as judge-made law, case law or common law.

president: the individual occupying the office in which the US *Constitution* vests sole executive power.

● The Constitution states that the president be at least 35 years old and a natural born citizen who has been resident in the USA for 14 years.

● The president is afforded a range of domestic and foreign policy powers under the Constitution.

■ *e.g.* In foreign policy the president is given the title of commander-in-chief of the armed forces. He is also empowered to negotiate *treaties* on behalf of the USA and nominate ambassadors.

■ *TIP* Though the constitutional powers of the president are considerable, much rests on the abilities of the incumbent. As President *Woodrow Wilson* concluded: 'The president is at liberty, both in law and in conscience, to be as big a man as he can. His capacity will set the limits.'

Presidential Daily Briefing (PDB): an intelligence document given to the *president* each morning by the director of national intelligence. Also known as the President's Daily Brief or the President's Daily Bulletin.

● The *vice-president* has also been given a copy of the PDB since *Walter Mondale*'s time in the post (1977–81).

presidential persuasion: see *Richard Neustadt*.

presidential primaries: see *primaries*.

presidential support score: first published in 1953, a statistical measure of a president's legislative success rate. It is expressed as a percentage calculated on the basis of how often a president's clearly stated positions on policy are mirrored by recorded votes in the *House* and *Senate*.

▦ *e.g.* In 1995 *Bill Clinton*'s presidential support score was only 36.2%. This was the first year of *divided government* following the Republican successes in the 1994 *mid-term elections*.

presidential wars: refers to the president's use of his power as commander-in-chief of the armed forces to wage war without a formal declaration by *Congress*. See *War Powers Act (1973)*.

Press Office: the body charged with managing relations between the *president* and the *media*. Located in the White House and headed by a director known as the press secretary.

▦ *e.g.* Tony Snow was *George W. Bush*'s press secretary in January 2007.

pressure group: a group of like-minded individuals who look to advance their shared sectional interests, or a cause they hold in common, by trying to influence those in power.

▦ *TIP* Political parties and pressure groups can be distinguished from one another by the fact that though the latter may sometimes put up candidates in elections as a means of raising their profile or pressurising the candidates of other parties, they have no desire to form a government.

primaries (primary elections): a type of 'pre-election' held by political parties as a means of selecting the candidates who will represent them in the election proper.

● Primaries proliferated in the USA after the 1968 *McGovern-Fraser Commission*. In most cases they were introduced as replacement for *caucuses*.

● Primaries differ from state to state.

▦ *e.g.* In some states all registered voters are entitled to vote in each party's primary. Such contests are known as open primaries. In other states primaries are closed, which means that voters have to be a registered supporter of a *party* in order to cast a ballot in that party's primary.

▦ *TIP* Though primaries were introduced as a means of increasing levels of political participation, some argue that they have contributed to party decline, as well as making elections more expensive and more *candidate-centred*.

▦ *COMPARATIVE* In the UK, the Conservative Party has experimented with the use of primaries as a means of selecting parliamentary candidates in some constituencies.

privacy: though the US *Constitution* did not clearly set out the extent to which individuals had a right to privacy, the *Supreme Court* established and defined a 'zone of privacy' in cases such as *Griswold* v *Connecticut (1965)* and *Roe* v *Wade (1973)*.

- This zone of privacy was rooted in *penumbras* emanating from the *First, Fourth, Fifth* and *Ninth Amendments*.

pro-choice: supporting a woman's right to choose whether or not she terminates her pregnancy by means of an *abortion*.

- There are a number of high profile pro-choice *pressure groups* in the USA.

■ *e.g.* the *National Abortion Rights Action League (NARAL)*.

pro-life: a term implying opposition to a range of practices including *abortion*, embryological research and euthanasia.

- A number of high profile evangelical pro-life groups were especially active in US politics in the 1980s and 1990s, e.g. the *Moral Majority* and the *Christian Coalition*.

Proposition 13 (1978): also known as the Jarvis-Gann initiative, Proposition 13 remains one of the most famous of all state-wide California initiatives. This measure cut property taxes in California by almost two-thirds in an attempt to force the state government into spending its budget surplus. The loss of revenue resulting from this measure in fact led to a massive budget crisis and the suspension of vital state services.

Proposition 187 (1994): a state-wide California initiative that sought to deny illegal immigrants access to public healthcare, social services and education provision.

- Though the measure passed with nearly 60% of the vote it was later struck down by a *federal court*.

protectional groups: see *interest groups*.

protectionist groups: see *interest groups*.

protest voting: where individuals opt to vote for a candidate representing a party that they would not normally support in order to send a message to their 'natural' party, or to the party in government.

- The domination of the two major parties in the USA makes it harder for citizens to cast a protest vote without it having a direct effect on the outcome of the election.

■ *e.g.* Some saw the marked support for *Ross Perot* in the 1992 presidential election as evidence of a sizeable protest vote amongst traditional Republican supporters against the incumbent Republican President *George H. W. Bush*.

■ *COMPARATIVE* In the UK, protest voting often takes place where the outcome of the election in question is less crucial to the voter, e.g. the LibDems achieved spectacularly impressive by-election results in supposedly safe Conservative seats towards then end of the Conservatives' 18-year spell in office (1979–97) and did similarly well in safe Labour seats in the decade that followed (1997–2007).

Quayle, Dan (1947–): *vice-president* to *George H. W. Bush* (1989–93). He was previously a member of the US *House of Representatives* (1977–81) and the *Senate* (1981–88).

- Despite some successes in piloting legislation through the Senate, Quayle was largely seen as an intellectual lightweight and figure of fun by the US *media*.
- *e.g.* the media coverage of Quayle misspelling the word 'potato' (he suggested 'potatoe') at a US 'spelling bee'.

quotas: in respect of minority representation, the practice of reserving a percentage of places for those from ethnic groups that have been disadvantaged historically.

- The use of quotas is closely associated with *affirmative action* (positive discrimination) programmes.
- *e.g.* In the late 1960s and early 1970s it became common for universities in some states to operate quotas when allocating undergraduate places.
- *TIP* In recent years the US *Supreme Court* has ruled the use of such mechanistic quotas *unconstitutional* in cases such as *Regents of the University of California v Bakke (1978)*.

Rankin v McPherson (1987): a case in which the US *Supreme Court* upheld the right of someone to express a desire to the see the *president* assassinated.

- 19-year-old clerk Ardith McPherson was sacked after he was overheard saying 'if they go for him [Reagan] again, I hope they get him'. McPherson's reported comments followed an attempt on President *Ronald Reagan*'s life in 1981.
- The Court ruled that McPherson should not have been sacked because he was acting within his *First Amendment* right to *freedom of speech*.
- **TIP** If the Court had defined what McPherson said as 'fighting words' (defined by the Court as words 'designed to harm emotionally or to trigger a hostile reaction'), this would have been an example of unprotected speech.

ratification: most commonly used to refer to the process by which a *treaty* concluded by the *president* is approved by two-thirds of the US *Senate*. It is also used where an amendment to the US *Constitution* is confirmed with the support of three-quarters of the (currently 38) states.

- **e.g.** The US Senate failed to ratify the Treaty of Versailles that President *Woodrow Wilson* had negotiated in 1919. The proposed *Equal Rights Amendment* to the US Constitution also failed, having only secured the support of 35 of the 38 states needed for ratification within the allotted time.

Rayburn, Sam (1882–1961): a long-serving former *Speaker of the House of Representatives*.

- **e.g.** Rayburn's advice to members of the *House of Representatives* was simply to 'vote your district' (i.e. take care of 'the folks back home').

Reagan, Ronald (1911–2004): a former Hollywood actor and later governor of *California*, Reagan served as the fortieth *president* of the USA, 1981–89.

- Reagan's election was widely seen as a victory for the *New Right*.
- His domestic policy focused on reducing the scale and scope of the federal government. He favoured deregulation in business, accompanied by cuts in personal taxation.
- These policies, known as 'Reaganomics', resulted in massive economic growth but also crippling budget deficits. In the 1980 presidential *primaries*, Reagan's rival (later his *vice-president*) *George H. W. Bush*, described Reagan's economic policy as 'voodoo economics'.

- In foreign policy Reagan was credited with ending the Cold War, having earlier pursued a policy of demonising the USSR (describing it as 'the Evil Empire'). He also bombed Libya, invaded Grenada, and launched the *Strategic Defense Initiative*.
- Reagan's foreign policy was overshadowed by the investigation into the *Iran-Contra affair*.

■ *TIP* Reagan became known as the 'Teflon President' because nothing ever stuck to him!

recall election: a recall is a procedure that allows registered voters in a state to petition to hold a public vote to remove an elected official from office before the end of his/her term.

- Around one in three US states offer this power to voters, though in practice such recalls are often difficult to execute.
- A recall petition normally has to secure the support of a predetermined number of votes before it qualifies for the ballot. In California, for example, a recall of a state-wide official such as the governor would require a number of signatures equal to at least 12% of the total votes cast in the last election for the office in question.
- In most cases recalls are only permitted where there is evidence of corruption, negligence or, in some cases, incompetence.

■ *e.g.* Those organising the 2003 recall of California Governor Gray Davis claimed that the Democrat had 'mismanaged state finances', 'threatened public safety by cutting services' and had been 'slacking-off' in his job, having allegedly 'gone two years without calling a cabinet meeting'. Davis lost the recall vote (55.3% to 44.7%) and was replaced by *Arnold Schwarzenegger* who won 48.7% of the vote in a field of 135 candidates.

■ *TIP* Though the recall process can make politicians more accountable to voters, it also undermines the principle of *representative democracy*, e.g. when the 'Recall Gray Davies' campaign was launched in February 2003, the governor was only weeks into his second term having been convincingly re-elected the previous November. There was even evidence that the campaign had been organised and funded by disgruntled Republicans.

reconstruction: commonly applied to the period from the end of the American *Civil War* (1865) until 1877 this term refers to the period of bridge-building and reconciliation between the victorious northern United States and the defeated former Confederate states in the south.

■ *e.g.* This period saw the *ratification* of the *Thirteenth Amendment* (1865), the *Fourteenth Amendment* (1865) and the *Fifteenth Amendment* (1870).

re-election rates: see *incumbency*.

referendum: a popular vote on a measure proposed or passed by a *legislature*, as opposed to a measure proposed by the people, which is known as an *initiative*.

- Though regulations vary from state to state, referendums generally take place where: the legislature decides to put a measure or policy to a public vote; the legislature is required by law to put certain measures to a public vote; or the people have the right to force a referendum on a law passed by the legislature by raising a petition carrying a predetermined number of signatures (a petition referendum).

- States such as California refer to referendums and other public votes as propositions and identify them by a number.

- *e.g.* In Proposition 48 (November 2002) California voters were asked to approve an amendment to the state's constitution that deleted all references to the level of municipal courts that had been removed by an earlier measure. The proposition was passed with the support of 72% of voters.

- *TIP* It is important to be able to distinguish between referendums and the power of initiative, which is available to citizens in some US states.

- *COMPARATIVE* In the 1940s, Labour Prime Minister Clement Attlee described referendums as 'devices alien to our traditions'. Though there have been a number of referendums in the UK since the 1970s there was only one UK-wide referendum between 1973 and 2007. Some argue that this unwillingness to use such devices more widely results from the fact that the UK is a *representative democracy.*

Reform Party: founded by *Ross Perot* in 1995 and closely associated with his independent candidacies in the 1992 and 1996 presidential elections.

- The party was founded to provide voters with a 'Washington outsider' alternative to the two major parties.

- *Jesse Ventura*, the former pro-wrestler and one-term independent governor of Minnesota was initially a Reform Party candidate.

- The party suffered as a result of the infighting that accompanied *Pat Buchanan*'s capture of the party's nomination in the 2000 presidential election.

Regents of the University of California v Bakke (1978): a case in which the US *Supreme Court* ruled that a university's use of racial *quotas* violated the *Fourteenth Amendment* by applying reverse discrimination. Such quotas had been used widely as an element of many *affirmative action* programmes.

- Alan Bakke was a white male who wanted to study medicine. His applications to the University of California Medical School at Davis were rejected in 1972 and 1973, despite the fact that he was better qualified on paper than some of those non-white students admitted to the course under the school's affirmative action programme.

- The Court ruled that Bakke had been denied the equal protection under the law demanded by the Fourteenth Amendment and that he should be admitted to Davis. He graduated from the school in 1982.

- *TIP* Though the Bakke case invalidated the kinds of mechanistic quotas used by the University of California, it did not rule out the possibility that race might be taken into consideration as an 'access-factor' when deciding between applicants.

Rehnquist, William H. (1924–2005): a chief justice of the US *Supreme Court*, 1986–2005 ,who had earlier served as an associate justice on the Court, 1971–86.

● He was appointed associate justice by *Richard Nixon* (confirmed 68:26 in the *Senate*) and promoted to the position of chief justice by *Ronald Reagan* (confirmed 65:33).

● Seen as a *strict constructionist*, Rehnquist was a keen advocate of state rights.

● Rehnquist's death in 2005 saw the appointment of *John Roberts* as chief justice.

▓ *e.g.* In cases such as *Webster* v *Reproductive Health Services (1989)* Rehnquist voted to uphold the constitutionality of state laws that restricted the availability of *abortion*.

▓ *TIP* In his last decade on the Court Rehnquist, *Clarence Thomas* and *Antonin Scalia* formed a solid conservative block that was often joined by *Anthony Kennedy*.

reinforcement theory: the belief that the *media*, rather than changing minds, simply reinforces those beliefs and opinions that individuals already hold.

Reno, Janet (1938–): served in the Clinton *cabinet* between 1993 and 2001 as the first female US attorney general.

● Reno is closely associated with the investigation into the botched Federal Bureau of Investigations/Bureau of Alcohol, Tobacco and Firearms siege of the *Branch Davidians'* compound at Waco, Texas, in 1993.

● Her position as attorney general meant that she was also named as the plaintiff in a number of significant *Supreme Court* cases concerning civil liberties.

▓ *e.g.* Reno v American Civil Liberties Union (1997).

***Reno* v *American Civil Liberties Union* (1997):** a case in which the US *Supreme Court* struck down two provisions of the Communications Decency Act (1996), which had sought to protect minors from harmful material available on the internet.

● The Court ruled (7:2) that though creating 'adult only zones' on the internet was not always *unconstitutional* in itself, the method used in the offending Act violated the *First Amendment* protection of *freedom of speech*.

representative democracy: the principle that although citizens elect politicians to represent their interests in government, those elected are not delegates sent with specific instructions or orders to follow. As a result, legislators may well make decisions that are contrary to the wishes of those who voted them into office.

● The principle of representative democracy is closely linked to notions of *popular sovereignty* and to the ideas of Edmund Burke. As a result, some refer to representative democracy as the Burkeian model of democracy.

▓ *e.g.* In a speech to his Bristol constituents in 1774, Edmund Burke summed up what many see as the essence of representative democracy: 'Your representative owes you not his industry only but his judgement; and he betrays you if he sacrifices it to your opinion.'

TIP Some argue that *referendums* and other forms of *direct democracy* undermine our system of representative democracy. If we elect representatives to act in our best interests, it is argued, they should not feel obliged to seek our approval for a specific policy at a later date. Politicians must be free to implement the policies that they judge necessary between one election and the next. See *mandate*.

republicanism: a style of government that places great emphasis on individual liberty, citizenship, and the *rule of law* whilst at the same time eschewing monarchy and aristocracy.

Republican National Committee (RNC): first established in 1856, the RNC is the national body that oversees the organisation of the *Republican Party*, plans the *party convention* in presidential election years, and helps to coordinate the party's electoral efforts between presidential elections.

- The RNC is appointed by the party's quadrennial presidential nominating convention and is headed by a chair.

e.g. In 2007 the RNC was chaired by Mike Duncan.

Republican Party: formed in 1854 and often referred to as the *Grand Old Party (GOP)*, the Republican Party is one of the two major parties operating in the USA.

- The party had its origins in the northern, anti-slavery factions of the two main parties of that time; the Democrats and the Whigs.
- The Party has traditionally fared far better in presidential elections than in those for the *legislature*.

e.g. 18 Republican presidents served between the election of the party's first president, *Abraham Lincoln* (1861), and 2007. In the same period there were only 10 Democrat presidents, though Democrat *Franklin D. Roosevelt* was elected for four consecutive terms in 1932, 1936, 1940 and 1944.

reserved powers: see *Tenth Amendment*.

revolving-door syndrome: the way in which individuals in *Congress* or in the *executive* leave elected office to take up well-paid consultancy jobs with special *interest groups*, whilst former consultants find themselves being offered key positions in the administration of the day.

- Critics argue that such cross-over in personnel makes it difficult for government agencies such as the *Independent Regulatory Commission* to perform their regulatory function effectively.

e.g. According to the *Guardian*, Robert Rubin, Clinton's Treasury chief, later became a senior figure at *Enron* creditors Citigroup where he lobbied the Bush administration on behalf of Enron.

TIP Such practices are closely linked to the concept of *iron triangles*.

Rhode Island: the thirteenth state; joined the *Union* in 1790.

- Rhode Island was the only one of the former British colonies not to send delegates to the *Philadelphia Constitutional Convention* in 1787. It was also the last of the 13 to ratify the *Constitution* agreed at the Convention.

Rice, Condoleezza (1954–): US secretary of state during President *George W. Bush*'s second term having been *national security advisor* (NSA) during the first.

- Rice had earlier been a foreign policy advisor to *George H. W. Bush* and a professor of political science at Stanford University.

rider: see *pork-barrelled bill*.

rights: philosophers such as *John Locke* identified what they referred to as 'natural rights'; universal, God-given, and inalienable rights to things such as life, liberty and property. Such ideas have been echoed in documents such as the US *Declaration of Independence* (1776).

- A belief in 'natural rights' rests on a concept of a 'natural human state' that predates not only political institutions but also society itself.
- As a result, the term 'rights' is now more commonly used to refer to the legal entitlement to have or do something, as granted by the state to its citizens.
- See *Bill of Rights* and *positive rights*.

right to life: a fundamental right most famously asserted in *Thomas Jefferson*'s opening sentence to the 1776 *Declaration of Independence*: 'We hold these truths to be self-evident, that all men are created equal, that they are endowed by their Creator with certain unalienable Rights, that among these are Life, Liberty and the pursuit of Happiness.'

- The right to life is explicitly protected by a number of passages in the US *Constitution* as well as numerous congressional laws.
- *e.g.* The *Fifth Amendment* prohibits the taking of an individual's 'life, liberty, or property, without *due process of law*'.
- *TIP* The concept of the right to life and the debate over what precisely constitutes 'life' has been at the centre of the debate over whether practices such as *abortion* and euthanasia are permissible under the Constitution.

Ring v Arizona (2002): a case in which the US *Supreme Court* ruled that death sentences imposed by a judge as opposed to a jury violated the *Sixth Amendment*'s guarantee of a trial by jury.

Rivers, L. Mendel (1905–70): a member of the US *House of Representatives* for nearly 30 years representing South Carolina. Chairman of the House Committee on Armed Services between 1965 and 1970.

- Rivers is said to be an excellent example of a senior House Member who took care of 'the folks back home' by winning federal government contracts and other benefits for his state whilst chairman of the House Committee on Armed Services.
- *e.g.* Rivers was said to have gained 11 major new naval installations for his state (ship yards, missile bases, hospitals and training camps). The Bureau of Naval Personnel and the Naval Reserve Headquarters were also all moved to South Carolina. According to David S. Sorenson, 'it was said of L. Mendel Rivers that if he located one more base near Charleston, the whole district would sink into the sea'.

■ *TIP* The term 'pork' is used to describe the federal government contracts and subsidies that members of the US *Congress* look to win for their *districts* or states. See *pork-barrelled bill.*

RNC: see *Republican National Committee.*

Roberts, John (1955–): appointed US *Supreme Court* chief justice in 2005 following the death of *William H. Rehnquist.* He was nominated by *George W. Bush* and confirmed by the *Senate,* 78:22.

● Roberts's nomination was relatively uncontroversial. First, he was regarded as a capable, if relatively inexperienced, Appeals Court judge. Second, the replacement of Rehnquist with Roberts was widely seen as a 'like-for-like' change, as both men were viewed as conservatives (or '*strict constructionists*'). The appointment was therefore unlikely to affect the overall balance of the Court.

■ *TIP* Roberts was only 50 at the time of his appointment as chief justice. This is significant as he might reasonably be expected to serve in the post for 20 or 30 years.

***Roe* v *Wade* (1973):** a landmark case that saw the US *Supreme Court* asserting a woman's constitutional right to *abortion* (5:4).

● 'Roe' was the pseudonym of the plaintiff, *Norma McCorvey.* Henry Wade was the criminal district attorney for Dallas County, Texas. McCorvey had been denied an abortion because under Texas law such a procedure was only permitted in order to save a mother's life.

● A constitutional protection of privacy had already been established in cases such as *Griswold* v *Connecticut (1965).* The *Roe* verdict extended this zone of privacy to cover abortion, whilst accepting that the balance between the mother's right to privacy and the foetus's right to life would alter as the pregnancy progressed (see *trimester*).

■ *TIP* The *Roe* case is an excellent example of *judicial review* and is often used as evidence of *judicial activism.* With the *Constitution* making no explicit reference to abortion, the Court interpreted certain key passages (e.g. the *Ninth Amendment*) in order to extend its meaning (see *penumbras*).

rogue elector (or 'faithless elector')**:** a member of the US *Electoral College* who casts his/her vote for a candidate other than the one whom he/she was sent to support by his/her state.

■ *e.g.* In 2000 one of the three Electoral College members representing Washington DC, Barbara Lett-Simmons, abstained in protest at the capital's lack of voting rights in *Congress.* She was supposed to cast her ballot for the *Democratic Party ticket* of *Al Gore* and *Joe Lieberman.*

■ *TIP* Though over 20 states have laws to punish rogue electors after the event, there is little they can do to stop such behaviour. This is a result of the power vested in members of the Electoral College by the US *Constitution.*

roll call vote: normally refers to a recorded vote in the US *Senate* where the names of Senators are called out in alphabetical order and members formally indicate their support for, or opposition to, a measure.

r

- Most non-controversial votes in the Senate are taken as simple voice-votes where members call out 'aye' or 'no' when prompted.
- Roll call votes are normally used when the issue at hand is considered contentious or when at least one-fifth of those Senators present consider it advantageous to have the names of those voting for and against a measure recorded.
- ■ *TIP* Recorded votes in the *House of Representatives* were also done by roll call prior to the introduction of electronic voting in the chamber.

Roosevelt, Franklin Delano (1882–1945): the thirty-second US *president* who served from 1933 until his death in 1945. Roosevelt is often referred to simply by his initials, FDR.

- Roosevelt was elected for a record four consecutive terms as president (in 1932, 1936, 1940 and 1944). The length of his tenure was said to be one of the factors that prompted the *ratification* of the *Twenty-Second Amendment* in 1951.
- Roosevelt's time in office is most often remembered for the *New Deal* programme that his administration introduced in order to cope with the effects of the *Great Depression*. He also led the USA into the Second World War following the Japanese attack on Pearl Harbor in 1941.

Roosevelt, Theodore (1858–1919): the twenty-sixth US *president*, 1901–09.

***Roper* v *Simmons* (2005):** a case in which the US *Supreme Court* ruled as *unconstitutional* the execution of anyone under the age of 18 at the time the offence in question took place.

Rousseau, Jean Jacques (1712–78): an eighteenth-century Genevan philosopher best known for his 1762 book, *The Social Contract*.

- Rousseau's ideas influenced both the French Revolution and — along with other social contract theorists such as *John Locke* — the *Founding Fathers*.
- His work is closely linked with the concept of *popular sovereignty*.

Rove, Karl (1950–): a political consultant and White House deputy *chief of staff* under *George W. Bush*. He masterminded Bush's 2000 and 2004 presidential election victories.

- Rove is strongly associated with the use of high-level, targeted marketing techniques to 'build up' or 'energise' the base (see *building up the base*).
- ■ *COMPARATIVE* Consultants working for the UK Conservative Party spoke to Rove's team before the 2005 UK general election. Their campaign, coordinated by Australian consultant Lynton Crosby, used tactics similar to those employed in the USA by Rove in an effort to ensure the loyalty of the party's core supporters.

Ruby Ridge: refers to a siege at a hillside location in North Idaho in 1992.

- Alleged white separatist Randy Weaver had failed to appear in court to face charges that he had supplied an undercover informant with a sawn-off shotgun. Agents of the Bureau of Alcohol, Tobacco and Firearms (ATF) surrounded the home of Randy Weaver and his family. Weaver's son (14), his wife and a US marshall were killed when shooting broke out.

- Weaver was ultimately acquitted of supplying the shotgun (on grounds of entrapment) and of murdering a US marshall (on grounds of self-defence). The surviving members of the Weaver family were eventually awarded significant damages as a result of a wrongful death suit.
- **TIP** Events at Ruby Ridge and *Waco* were said to have motivated those who planned the *Oklahoma Bombing*.

rule of law: the principle that governments can only exercise legitimate *authority* when they work within the published laws and accept established procedure.

- It is commonly seen as an attempt to challenge arbitrary government.
- A. V. Dicey identified three strands of the rule of law in his book, *An Introduction to the Study of the Law of the Constitution* (1885): first, that no man can be punished without trial; second, that no one is above the law and all are subject to the same justice; and third, that the general principles of the *Constitution* (e.g. personal freedoms) result from the decisions of judges (case law) rather than from statute or executive order.
- The rule of law was traditionally said to be at the heart of the US and UK systems of government.
- **TIP** Some argue that the measures introduced in the wake of *9/11* have undermined the rule of law, in both the UK and the USA.
- **e.g.** the way in which some of those individuals suspected of involvement in terrorism were detained indefinitely without being charged (indicted) or tried.

Rules Committee: a committee in the *House of Representatives* that plays a key role in setting the rules of debate and amendment pertaining to each bill that comes before the House.

- Once a *standing committee* has reported a bill back out to the House it must be placed on the *calendar* for its second reading.
- Most bills are passed to the Rules Committee where they are given a 'rule' that stipulates the date on which they are to be heard and the degree of debate and amendment that they will be subject to.
- **e.g.** The Committee can assign a bill one of three types of 'rule': an open rule allows the bill to be amended without limits; a closed rule restricts the amendments that can be passed; and a special rule demands that the House consider the bill immediately.
- As is the case with other standing committees, the Rules Committee can *pigeonhole* a bill, though the House can force the Committee to release a bill by passing a 'discharge petition' with a simple majority.
- **TIP** The Rules Committee is often referred to as the 'traffic cop' of *Congress*. Professor William H. Riker preferred to describe the Committee as 'a toll bridge attendant who argues and bargains with each prospective customer: who lets his friends go free, who will not let his enemies pass at any price'.

Rumsfeld, Donald (1932–): a former member of the US *House of Representatives* and later advisor to *Richard Nixon*, Rumsfeld is best known for his two nonconsecutive terms as US secretary of defense, first under President *Gerald Ford* (1975–77) and later under *George W. Bush* (2001–06).

- Rumsfeld was a key figure in planning and coordinating the US response to *9/11*, specifically the attacks on Afghanistan and Iraq.
- He was widely regarded as one of the foreign policy 'hawks' in George W. Bush's inner circle. He was said to have clashed with George W. Bush's first-term secretary of state, *Colin Powell*, over the *War on Terror*.
- **TIP** Rumsfeld resigned in the wake of the Republicans' losses in the 2006 *mid-term elections*, which were widely seen as a consequence of the administration's failures over Iraq.

running mate: the candidate running for the post of *vice-president* in the quadrennial presidential election; the other half of the '*ticket*'.

- Though the *party conventions* once played a key role in choosing their vice-presidential candidates, the choice is now more often made by the parties' presidential nominee.
- There is still often an effort to 'balance the ticket' in terms of geography (Kennedy–Johnson), age (Kerry–Edwards) or experience (Bush–Cheney).
- **TIP** The choice of running mate can prove important in the election proper. *George W. Bush*'s choice of the experienced *Dick Cheney* was seen as a way of reassuring those who felt that Bush lacked the experience or the ability to be president. *George H. W. Bush*'s decision to stick with incumbent vice-president *Dan Quayle* as his running mate proved more problematic.
- **COMPARATIVE** In the UK, there is a similar phenomenon with the emergence of the role of deputy prime minister, and/or deputy party leader. Working class 'old Labour' John Prescott, for example, was seen as a balance to Fettes and Oxbridge-educated, New Labour Blair.

SALT: see *Strategic Arms Limitation Talks*.

Sanders, Bernie (1941–): a democratic socialist and independent member of the US *Senate* representing Vermont in the 110th *Congress*. Sanders previously represented Vermont in the US *House of Representatives*.

- Sanders won the Senate seat vacated by the departing independent (formerly Republican) Senator *James Jeffords*.
- Although Sanders was elected as an independent he *caucuses* with the Democrats in the Senate.

Scalia, Antonin (1936–): an associate justice of the US *Supreme Court* nominated by President *Ronald Reagan* in 1986.

- A *strict constructionist* on the conservative wing of the Court, Scalia has championed the concept of original intent when interpreting the US *Constitution*.
- Scalia, a committed Roman Catholic with nine children, is critical of the Court's 1973 *Roe* v *Wade* ruling on *abortion* and has looked to limit the availability of the practice.

■ *e.g.* In cases such as *Webster* v *Reproductive Health Services (1989)* Scalia voted in favour of the constitutionality of state laws that restricted the availability of abortion.

Schlesinger (jr.), Arthur (1917–2007): historian and presidential advisor best known for popularising the term 'the imperial presidency' in his 1973 book of the same name. See *imperial presidency*.

- Schlesinger served as an advisor to a number of presidents including *John F. Kennedy*.

School District of Abington Township v Schempp (1963): a case in which the US *Supreme Court* ruled that although the study of religion could be part of the school curriculum, prayer in publicly funded schools was barred under the *First Amendment's* Establishment Clause.

Schwarzenegger, Arnold (1947–): a former body-builder turned actor who was elected as governor of California for the *Republican Party* as a result of the 2003 *recall election* that removed the then incumbent Democrat Gray Davis. Schwarzenegger was elected for a second term in 2006.

- Schwarzenegger cannot become US *president* as he is not a natural born citizen. He was born in Austria and only became a US citizen in 1983.

scrutiny: see *oversight.*

SDI: see *Strategic Defense Initiative.*

Second Amendment (1791): one of ten amendments, known collectively as the *Bill of Rights*, the Second Amendment explicitly entrenches the right to bear arms. It asserts that 'A well regulated Militia, being necessary to the security of a free State, the right of the people to keep and bear Arms, shall not be infringed'.

- Some critics believe that wording of the Amendment makes the right to bear arms dependent upon the historic need for a 'well regulated militia' in the post-colonial period. As a result, they argue, the Amendment is anachronistic and should no longer be applied.
- Efforts to place restrictions on the free availability of handguns in the USA have, however, often been struck down by the *Supreme Court* as a result of challenges brought under the Second Amendment. See *Brady Bill.*
- Any changes to, or the repeal of, the Second Amendment would necessitate a constitutional amendment requiring the support of three-quarters of states. This is unlikely as there will almost certainly always be 13 or more states that would prefer to retain the Amendment in its present form.
- ▦ *COMPARATIVE* In the UK, it was possible to bring in an outright ban on handguns by the means of a simple Act of Parliament, passed in the wake of the murder of a teacher and 16 school children at a school in Dunblane in March 1996.
- ▦ *TIP* The relative ease with which controls on handguns were introduced in the UK as compared to the USA provides a good illustration of the difference between *entrenched* and unentrenched rights.

sectional groups: see *interest groups.*

security of tenure: where individuals are appointed to a post on a permanent basis, subject only to their good behaviour. Said to be a key condition of judicial independence.

- The term is most often used with reference to US *Supreme Court* justices who can only be forcibly removed through the *impeachment* process.
- ▦ *e.g.* The only Supreme Court justice to be impeached was Samuel Chase in 1805. He was not convicted and remained a member of the Court until his death in 1811.
- ▦ *TIP* The impeachment process was not intended as a means by which justices could be removed for political reasons. It should only be employed in cases of high crimes or misdemeanours.
- ▦ *COMPARATIVE* Senior UK judges also benefit from security of tenure.

select committee: an investigative committee most often created on an ad hoc basis to deal with a scandal or emergency, e.g. the joint select committee on the *Iran-Contra affair.*

- Select committees in the US are sometimes referred to as special committees.
- Though most select committees are temporary, some are permanent, e.g. the House Permanent Select Committee on Intelligence.
- ▣ *TIP* Though many select committees are created to deal with issues that are beyond the scope of any of the permanent *standing committees* present in the US *Congress*, they may also be created where the issue at hand would be likely to take up too much of the relevant standing committee's time.
- ▣ *COMPARATIVE* In the UK, the term select committee is normally used to refer to the departmental select committees created to scrutinise the work of government departments after 1979.

Senate: the smaller of the two chambers in the US *legislature*. It comprises 100 members, two for each of the 50 US states.

- The equal representation of the various states in the Senate is a result of the historic *Connecticut Compromise* that also saw the *House of Representatives* apportioned in broad proportion to population.
- The members of the US Senate were appointed by their respective state legislatures (under Article 1, section 3 of the US *Constitution*) until the *Seventeenth Amendment* (1913) introduced direct elections by the people.
- The fact that there are relatively few members in the chamber (only 100 compared to the 435 in the House of Representatives) means that debate is far more relaxed. This gives rise to senatorial privileges such as the right to *filibuster*.
- The Senate shares co-equal legislative power with the House of Representatives but it has exclusive power in respect of ratifying *treaties* (with a two-thirds majority) and confirming presidential appointments (with a simple majority).
- ▣ *e.g.* The Senate refused to ratify the Treaty of Versailles (1919) and also rejected *Ronald Reagan*'s nomination of *Robert Bork* to the US *Supreme Court* in 1987.
- ▣ *TIP* Though it shares co-equal legislative power with the House of Representatives, the Senate is generally seen as the senior chamber in the US *Congress*, with many House Members eventually becoming Senators and few moving in the other direction. This is partly as a result of the exclusivity engendered by its small size and partly as a result of the more stringent entry requirements.
- ▣ *COMPARATIVE* In the UK, the unelected House of Lords has traditionally been seen as a revising chamber rather than body sharing co-equal legislative power with the Commons. This relationship was retained under the proposals for Lords reform unveiled by the government in 2007.

seniority rule: that the chair of each congressional *standing committee* is held by the member of the majority party with the longest continuous period of service on each committee. It is sometimes referred to, ironically, as the 'senility rule'.

- The rule was also applied to the position of 'ranking minority' member in each committee.
- ▣ *TIP* Though the use of secret ballots has become more widespread in the selection of such individuals in recent years, it is often the case that those elected are still those with the longest period of continuous service.

separation of powers: a doctrine requiring the three elements of government power — executive power, the legislative power and judicial power — to be held by separate branches of government as a means of avoiding tyranny.

- The term was developed by the philosopher Charles Louis de Secondat Montesquieu, Baron de la Brède (1689–1755) — commonly known as *Baron de Montesquieu* — in his 1748 work, *The Spirit of the Laws*.
- The *executive* branch has the role of executing policy (i.e. putting the laws into effect), the *legislature* has the role of legislating (i.e. making the laws), and the *judiciary* has the role of enforcing and interpreting the laws.
- This doctrine of separation of powers was a major consideration for those framing the US *Constitution* in 1787.
- **e.g.** Under the Constitution no individual can hold office in more than one of the three branches simultaneously. *John Kerry*, the *Democratic Party* presidential candidate in 2004 would therefore have had to give up his seat in the US *Senate* if he had been elected as *president*.
- **TIP** It would be impossible for any state to operate under a total separation of powers. In reality, therefore, *Richard Neustadt* was probably more accurate when he described the US system as having 'separated institutions, sharing powers'.
- **COMPARATIVE** The UK has traditionally been said to demonstrate 'fused' as opposed to separated powers. The executive is drawn from the legislature and the Lord Chancellor was traditionally a member of all three branches. The Constitutional Reform Act (2005) goes some way towards providing a clearer separation of powers in the UK, e.g. through the creation of a Supreme Court that is wholly separate from the House of Lords.

September 11, 2001: see *9/11*.

Seventeenth Amendment (1913): introduced direct elections to the US *Senate*.

- Under Article 1, section 3 of the US *Constitution* each state's members in the US Senate had previously been chosen by the state's own *legislature*.
- **TIP** It is commonly argued that the extensive powers afforded to the Senate are made more legitimate by the fact that its members are elected to office. Though this is true today, it is useful to know that the chamber's powers predate the popular election of its members.

Seventh Amendment (1791): preserves the right to trial by jury in all cases in common law where the sum in question is in excess of $20. It also prevents such cases being re-examined in any US court, unless allowed under common law.

Schumer, Charles (1950–): chair of the Democratic Senatorial Campaign Committee in 2006, elected vice-chair of Senate Democratic *caucus* in November 2006. Schumer was credited with playing a part in the Democrats' 2006 *mid-term election* successes in the *Senate*.

Sierra Club: a grass-roots environmental *pressure group* founded in California in 1892. The Sierra Club boasted over 700,000 members by 2005.

S

- The group helped to bring about the establishment of national parks such as Yosemite and Yellowstone, and also lobbied in favour of enactment of the *Clean Air Acts*.
- The group organises social functions and coordinates campaigns with like-minded organisations.
- In 2006 the group was campaigning on a range of issues including global warming and improved air quality.

signing statement: written statement released by the *president* at the same time as he signs a bill passed by *Congress* into law.

- Such statements were once relatively uncontroversial as they were simply used as a way of thanking all of those involved for the work they had done in making the law a reality.
- In recent years, however, presidents have used such statements both as a way of voicing their personal reservations regarding some elements of the legislation passed, and as a way of setting out how the new legislation should be applied and interpreted by *executive agencies* and others.
- Signing statements are controversial because the president often appears to be asserting his prerogative not to implement part of the legislation he is signing into law, as opposed to simply giving his opinion.
- **e.g.** In December 2005 *George W. Bush* added a statement that asserted his right to authorise torture, where he felt that such interrogation might prevent terrorist attacks, to a measure that imposed a blanket-ban on torture. This was one of more than 750 such statements that Bush issued between 2001 and 2006.
- Congress has seen such statements as an attack on its legislative *authority*. In 2006 Senator Arlen Spector sponsored a Presidential Signing Statement Act that demanded that: 'No state or federal court shall rely on or defer to a presidential signing statement as a source of authority.'
- **TIP** Some commentators argue that signing statements have become a form of de facto *line-item veto*. Others see the use of signing statements as a way in which the president can assert the power of what *John Yoo* and others have called the *unitary executive*.

simple plurality (simple majority): the largest single share of votes in a given election. Not necessarily an overall majority (absolute majority) of the total number of ballots cast.

- The *first-past-the-post* electoral system is often referred to as a simple plurality system.

Sixteenth Amendment (1913): granted *Congress* the power to levy a federal income tax.

- **TIP** This amendment overturned the *Supreme Court*'s ruling in *Pollock v Farmers' Loan and Trust Company (1895)*.

Sixth Amendment (1791): the sixth of ten amendments known collectively as the *Bill of Rights*. It guaranteed the right to a 'speedy and public trial...by an impartial jury'.

- The amendment also guaranteed the accused a number of other important rights, significantly: the right to legal council; the right to be made fully aware of any charges brought; the right to see prosecution witnesses, and also to subpoena witnesses in their defence.

Skull and Bones Society: a secret society based at Yale University (formally The Order of Skull and Bones).

- Though the organisation is highly secretive it is known to retain a fairly exclusive membership and to favour quasi-masonic rituals. In common with other secret societies, Skull and Bones is said to bind its members to further the group's collective interests within society.

■ *e.g.* Both of the main candidates in the 2004 presidential election — *John Kerry* (Democrat) and *George W. Bush* (Republican) — were members of Skull and Bones during their time at Yale.

slavery: a condition of involuntary servitude institutionalised in many southern US states in the nineteenth century.

- Opposition to slavery and the fear that the practice might spread into the northern United States following the *Supreme Court*'s historic *Dred Scott* v *Sandford* case in 1857 was a major cause of the *Civil War*.
- During the Civil War, President *Abraham Lincoln* issued the Emancipation Proclamation freeing all slaves in the *Confederacy* and thereby depriving the Confederate Army of a valuable source of manpower.
- Slavery was abolished by the *Thirteenth Amendment*, which was ratified in 1865, the year that the Confederate states were defeated.

■ *TIP* The Republican President Lincoln's historic role in the defeat of the South and abolition of slavery resulted in *Democratic Party* hegemony in the southern states for decades after the end of the conflict, a time when Americans were said to 'vote as they shot'. The 'Party of Lincoln', as the Republicans became known, was unable to make significant inroads into this *Solid South* until the 1960s.

smoke-filled rooms: dating from the 1920s, a term referring to the rooms in which political power-brokers meet secretly to make decisions.

- The term is closely associated with the *machine politics* of the 1950s with its '*fat cat*' party bosses.

soft money: money unregulated under the *Federal Election Campaign Act (1974)* following a 1979 exemption that allowed spending on party-building activities such as *voter registration drives* and *get out the vote campaigns*.

- Some groups also used such unregulated money in *issue advocacy* campaigns.
- Soft money was outlawed under the *Bipartisan Campaign Finance Reform Act of 2002 (BCRA)*.

■ *TIP* Prior to the BCRA, soft money contributions had come to dwarf the regulated *hard money* donations.

Solid South: characterising the *Democratic Party*'s electoral success in the southern states in the years between the end of the *Civil War* and the early 1960s.

S

- The phenomenon was said to be a result of the *Republican Party*'s historic role in defeating the Confederate states and abolishing *slavery*. As a result, 'the Party of Lincoln' found it hard to make electoral headway in the South.
- In recent years, however, the South has voted fairly solidly for Republicans in presidential elections.
- Some see this change in voting behaviour as a result in part of the Democrats' role in passing legislation such as the *1964 Civil Rights Act*. The *Southern Strategy* adopted by the Republicans towards the end of the 1960s may also have contributed to this trend.
- *e.g.* In the 1960 elections 99 of the 106 House Members and all 22 Senators returned from southern states were Democrat, as were all 11 of these states' governors.

son of Star Wars: see *Strategic Defense Initiative*.

Souter, David (1939–): an associate justice of the *Supreme Court* nominated by *George H. W. Bush* in 1990. Souter is generally regarded as being at the centre of the Court in terms of his jurisprudence.

South Carolina: the eighth state; joined the *Union* in 1788.

South Dakota: the fortieth state; joined the *Union* in 1889.

Southern Strategy: refers to the efforts of the Republicans to win presidential elections by appealing to socially conservative Democrat voters in the *Solid South*.

- The strategy is closely associated with *Richard Nixon*'s 1968 presidential election campaign.
- Some argue that the strategy was undermined by the independent candidacy of *George Wallace*.

sovereignty: the right to exercise supreme power within a given territory.

- In the USA, sovereignty is said to lie with the people (*popular sovereignty*) or with the *Constitution* (*constitutional sovereignty*).
- **COMPARATIVE** In the UK, Parliament was traditionally said to be sovereign (parliamentary sovereignty).

Speaker of the House of Representatives: a political figure who is elected by, and acts as a leader of, the majority party in the chamber. In 2007 the Speaker of the House was Democrat Nancy Pelosi, the first woman to hold the position.

- The Speaker is next in line to become *president* in the event that the president and *vice-president* are killed or incapacitated.
- They represent the House in meetings with the president.
- The Speaker will use his/her powers within the chamber in order to advance the interests of his/her party.
- *e.g.* The Speaker refers bills to committee, appoints select committee and conference committee chairs, influences the appointment of *standing committee* chairs, appoints the majority party contingent on the *House Rules Committee*, and presides over the House enforcing its rules.

▦ *TIP* Some see the US Speaker as being more akin to the UK prime minister than to the speaker of the House of Commons.

▦ *COMPARATIVE* The speaker of the House of Commons is expected to remain strictly impartial in the discharge of his/her duties. Consequently, the sitting speaker is technically an independent MP within the Commons and is re-elected in his/her constituency as 'the Speaker seeking re-election' rather than under his/her original party label.

special relationship: describes the close, historic links that exist between the USA and the UK culturally, politically and militarily.

● A special relationship particularly characterised the period from 1941 to the end of the Cold War in the 1990s.

▦ *e.g.* The cooperation evident during the Second World War or, more recently, in the actions in Iraq and Afghanistan.

▦ *TIP* Critics argue that the relationship is now taken rather more seriously by the UK government than by the USA.

split-ticket voting: where voters split their support between candidates of different parties running for different offices on a single election day.

● Split-ticket voting may result from a number of factors. In an age of *candidate-centred campaigns*, some voters appear less likely to be swayed by a party label alone. Some voters take the view that Republicans made better presidents, whereas Democrats made better *Congressmen*. Some voters split their tickets because they want to bring about 'divided' (and therefore more 'limited') government in Washington DC.

▦ *e.g.* In November 2004, voters in Colorado elected Democrat Ken Salazar to the US *Senate* at the same time that they voted to give *George W. Bush* a second term as US president.

▦ *TIP* Do not confuse split-ticket voting with swing. Voters' decision to return Clinton for a second term in 1996, at the same time that they left the *Republican Party* in control of both House and Senate, could be evidence of split-ticket voting; the Republican capture of *Congress* in the 1994 *mid-term elections*, following Clinton's victory in the 1992 presidential election, is not.

spoils system: the practice under which a victorious party in an election rewarded its supporters with government jobs (the 'spoils') by way of thanks for the work that they had done in the campaign.

● The system was brought into check by the *Pendleton Act (1883)* which introduced a more meritocratic system for appointments and promotions to most government posts.

square deal: refers collectively to the domestic policies of President *Theodore Roosevelt*.

● The epithet referred to the idea that there would be a fair (or 'square') deal between employers, employees and the general public.

S

standing committees: permanent committees in the *House* and the *Senate* that play a crucial role in scrutinising *executive departments* and *agencies* as well as considering legislative proposals.

- Standing committees have a virtual free-hand when considering bills. They can *pigeon-hole* bills, amend them as they see fit, or report them out to *Congress* unchanged.
- Committees are often described as 'little legislatures', the places where the real work of Congress is done. *Woodrow Wilson* described Congress in committee as 'Congress at work'.
- The role of the chairman within each committee is crucial.

■ *COMPARATIVE* US standing committees combine the roles performed by regular standing committees and departmental select committees in the UK. US standing committees are better financed, better staffed, and more powerful.

■ *e.g.* They have the power to subpoena witnesses.

START (Strategic Arms Reduction Talks): see *Strategic Arms Limitation Talks (SALT)*.

Star Wars: see *Strategic Defense Initiative*.

State Courts: those courts having original jurisdiction in most cases arising under state law.

- *Federal Courts* rather than State Courts have original jurisdiction in criminal and civil cases brought under federal statutes. Each state has at least one Federal Court alongside its various State Courts.
- Most states have a hierarchical judicial system consisting of a number of distinct tiers.

■ *e.g.* 95% of all cases in the USA are heard in State Trial Courts, the lowest tier of courts at the state level. Appeals from cases in these courts are normally heard in the State Intermediate Courts of Appeal. The highest court of appeal in most cases would be the State Supreme Court, though not all states have their own Supreme Court.

■ *TIP* Appeals from a State Supreme Court may pass to the US *Supreme Court* where federal law or the US *Constitution* has some bearing on the case, e.g. *Bush v Gore (2000)* came as a result of an appeal that followed a decision in the Florida Supreme Court.

State Department: the US *executive department* charged with the administration of foreign affairs. The Department is headed by a *cabinet*-level appointee, the secretary of state.

■ *e.g.* In 2007 the US secretary of state was *Condoleezza Rice*.

■ *TIP* There has been a history of tension between the State Department and the *National Security Council*.

■ *COMPARATIVE* The UK equivalent to the State Department is the Foreign Office.

state government: refers to the institutions established to govern at state level as opposed to those at the national (i.e. 'federal') government level.

- Individual states remain largely free to organise their own governments as a result of the *reserved powers* afforded them under the *Tenth Amendment*.
- As a result, the structure of state legislatures, the powers of state executives, and the terms of office for the various elected posts all vary from state to state.
- **e.g.** The state of Nebraska has a unicameral *legislature*, whereas all other US states operated under a *bicameral* system in 2007. Similarly, whereas 48 states elect their governors to 4-year terms, gubernatorial elections take place every 2 years in New Hampshire and Vermont.
- **TIP** It is important to remember that the federal government was created by the various states represented at the *Philadelphia Convention*. Thus, whilst it is technically possible for the states to amend the US *Constitution* without the consent of the US *Congress*, Congress cannot make such changes without the consent of three-quarters of states.

State of the Union Address: taken from a passage in Article 2, section 3 of the US *Constitution*, which states that 'The President shall from time to time give to the Congress Information of the State of the Union, and recommend to their consideration such measures as he shall judge necessary and expedient'.

- Nearly always occurring in January, the Address has come to be seen as an occasion on which the president sets out his legislative programme. It is widely seen as a feature of the president's extra-constitutional role as 'chief legislator'.
- **TIP** The legislative independence of *Congress* and the fact that the president is not guaranteed to have his own party in charge of either chamber means that the measures outlined in the State of the Union Address are by no means certain of finding their way into law.
- **COMPARATIVE** Parallels are often drawn between the State of the Union Address in the USA and the Queen's Speech in the UK.

Stevens, John Paul (1920–): an associate justice of the US *Supreme Court*. He was appointed by Republican President *Gerald Ford* in 1975, but is widely regarded as one of the more liberal-leaning justices on the Court.

- Still a member of the Court at the start of 2007, Stevens had served under three different chief justices: *Warren Burger, William Rehnquist* and *John Roberts*.

straight-ticket voting: where voters support all of the candidates standing for a particular party on election day, irrespective of the positions that they are contesting.

- **TIP** Straight-ticket voting is often contrasted with *split-ticket voting*.

Strategic Arms Limitation Talks (SALT): bilateral negotiations on nuclear weapons reduction that took place between the USA and the USSR during the Cold War.

- The talks resulted in two Strategic Arms Limitation Treaties (SALT I and SALT II).

- The later *Strategic Arms Reduction Talks (START)* led to the Strategic Arms Reduction Treaty of 1991 (START I) and a further agreement in 1993 (START II).
- **■ *TIP*** Although President *Jimmy Carter* signed SALT II, it was never formally ratified by the US *Senate*.

Strategic Arms Reduction Talks (START): see *Strategic Arms Limitation Talks (SALT)*.

Strategic Defense Initiative (SDI): known colloquially as 'Star Wars', SDI involved the planned deployment of satellite-based lasers that would destroy incoming intercontinental ballistic missiles whilst they were in the outer atmosphere.

- Technologically challenging and never fully realised, the SDI did play a part in bringing the USSR and USA together in talks over missile reduction. SDI also paved the way for a ground-based missile defence shield, sometimes referred to as 'son of Star Wars'.

Strickland v _Washington_ (1984): a case in which the US *Supreme Court* ruled that defendants have a right to a counsel whose performance is not defective to the point of altering the course of the trial.

strict constructionist: describes those *Supreme Court* justices who favour a literal interpretation of the *Constitution* and place an emphasis on the original intent of the *Founding Fathers*. See *loose constructionist*.

- **■ *e.g.*** Former Supreme Court Justice Hugo Black (see *Engel* v *Vitale*) and one-time Chief Justice *William H. Rehnquist* are notable strict constructionists.

sun-belt: a region covering most of the states in the south and southwestern regions of the USA.

- The sun-belt has seen a marked increase in population in recent years.
- Though some of this increase can be attributed to a movement from the *frost-belt* states, immigration into the southern United States from countries such as Mexico has also been a factor.
- **■ *e.g.*** The sun-belt includes states such as California, Florida, New Mexico and Texas.

sunshine rules: passed by the *House of Representatives* in 1973 and the *Senate* in 1975, these rules resulted in *congressional committees* doing most of their work in the full view of the public (i.e. in 'open session').

- Prior to these rules, committees had generally held 'hearings' in open session, with the more detailed examination of bills, the negotiations and the 'marking-up' process done in private session.
- The 'sunshine rules' were so called because they were seen to metaphorically throw open the doors of committee rooms, letting the light flood in.

Super Tuesday: a day every 4 years, traditionally in early March, when the largest number of US states hold their presidential *primaries*.

- **■ *e.g.*** In 2004 Super Tuesday took place on 2 March and involved contests in ten states.

■ **TIP** *Front-loading* has meant that Super Tuesday now often marks the day when each party's presidential nominee is all but decided, e.g. according to the *Economist*, *John Kerry's* victories in all ten of the *Democratic Party* primary contests held on Super Tuesday in 2004 meant that he 'woke up on March 3rd, with the Democratic nomination secure, to face the first barrage of television advertisements'.

Supreme Court: the highest appellate court in the USA (see *appellate jurisdiction*) and final arbiter of the meaning of the US *Constitution*. The Court also has original jurisdiction in certain cases, e.g. in cases where a US state is a party.

- The Court's size is controlled by *Congress*. Although it has been fixed at nine justices (one chief justice and eight associate justices) since an Act of 1869, it had previously ranged between six and ten members (see *court packing*).
- Justices have *security of tenure*. They are appointed for life — subject to good behaviour — and can only be removed through a process of *impeachment*.
- The president has the power to fill vacancies on the Court with the advice and consent of the *Senate*.
- Though the Court was established in Article 3 of the US Constitution its most important power — that of *judicial review* — was discovered by the Court itself in cases such as *Marbury* v *Madison (1803)*.

■ **COMPARATIVE** The Constitutional Reform Act (2005) established a timetable for the creation of a UK Supreme Court.

***Swann* v *Charlotte-Mecklenberg Board of Education* (1971):** a case in which the US *Supreme Court* ruled that de facto segregation was *unconstitutional*.

- De jure segregation, where state laws had explicitly separated students on the basis of race, had been declared unconstitutional under the *Fourteenth Amendment* in *Brown* v *Board of Education (1954)*.
- This ruling had not affected the areas where schools serving a particular neighbourhood were almost entirely 'black' or 'white' as a result of the local demography.
- The *Swann* case addressed this de facto ('in fact') segregation and led to the introduction of *bussing*.

swing states: those states upon which the outcome of an entire presidential election is said to hang.

- Most states award their entire allocation of *Electoral College* votes on a winner-takes-all basis. As a result, marginal victories in close states are far more important than they would be under a proportional system or a situation where the result was decided on the basis of the popular vote across the nation.
- Only three states changed hands between the presidential elections of 2000 and 2004.

■ **e.g.** The result of the 2000 presidential election depended upon the result in the key swing state of Florida, which *George W. Bush* eventually carried after the US *Supreme Court* called a halt to recounts (see *Bush* v *Gore*). In 2004 Ohio and Pennsylvania were said to be two of the key swing states.

■ *TIP* One should not underestimate the importance of such swing states. Had 120,000 voters in Ohio voted for *John Kerry* rather than Bush in 2004, Kerry would have won the Electoral College 272:266 with around 3,000,000 votes fewer than Bush nationally.

Symington Committee: a special committee set up by the Senate Foreign Relations Committee in February 1969 under the chairmanship of Stuart Symington (Missouri) to investigate secret US security agreements and commitments abroad.

● The committee's investigation uncovered a catalogue of presidential foreign policy abuses.

■ *e.g.* The *Nixon* administration had been fighting a secret air war in support of the Vientiane government against Pathet Lao in northern Laos since 1964, yet *Congress* believed that the bombing over Laos was against North Vietnamese troops passing along southeast Laos.

tactical voting: where a voter casts a ballot for an individual who is not his/her preferred candidate in order to prevent his/her least favourite candidate being elected. It is common under *simple plurality* systems such as *first-past-the-post* where there are more than two credible candidates.

● Tactical voting is not prevalent in the USA due to the overwhelming domination of the two main political parties.

■ *COMPARATIVE* The presence of a credible third party in the UK system and also the existence of a number of genuinely three-way or even four-way contests in individual constituencies makes tactical voting more of an option for voters.

Taft, William H. (1857–1930): the twenty-seventh US *president*, 1909–13.

Taylor, Zachary (1784–1850): the twelfth US *president*, 1849–50.

Tennessee: the sixteenth state; joined the *Union* in 1796.

Tenth Amendment (1791): protected the rights of individual US states by asserting the existence of so-called *reserved powers*, those powers that the *Constitution* neither explicitly delegates to the federal government nor bars the states from exercising.

■ *TIP* The US *Supreme Court* has been crucial in determining the extent of such reserved powers through its interpretation of the Constitution.

■ *COMPARATIVE* As the UK is a unitary state, Parliament retains the authority to vary the powers, suspend, or even abolish any unit of regional or local government.

tenure: see *security of tenure*.

term limits: a legal restriction imposed on the number of terms that an individual can serve in a named office.

● The introduction of term limits for *Congressmen* was a key plank in the Republicans' 1994 *Contract with American* platform.

● In both 1995 and 1997 the *House of Representatives* voted on proposals to introduce term limits by amending the US *Constitution*. Neither proposal secured the required two-thirds majority.

■ *e.g.* The US president is limited to two terms as a result of the *Twenty-Second Amendment* (1951).

Texas: the twenty-eighth state; joined the *Union* in 1845.

Texas v Johnson (1989): a case in which the US *Supreme Court* ruled that burning the American flag was a form of 'expressive conduct' protected as free speech under the *First Amendment* to the US *Constitution*.

● See *United States* v *Eichman (1990)* and *Flag Desecration Amendment*.

Third Amendment (1791): the first of ten amendments to the US *Constitution* that are known collectively as the *Bill of Rights*. It prevented soldiers from being quartered (i.e. billeted) in private houses in peacetime unless the owners gave their consent, and recognised legal limits on the quartering of soldiers in times of war.

third parties: refers to parties other than the Republicans and the Democrats.

● Third parties may operate at a national level (e.g. the *Reform Party*) or regional level (e.g. *George Wallace's American Independent Party*).

● Most third parties are temporary (e.g. *Strom Thurmond's* States Rights Party) but others are permanent (e.g. the *Green Party*).

● Some are issue-based (e.g. the Prohibition Party) whereas others are more ideological (e.g. the Socialist Party).

● The *simple plurality* electoral system makes life hard for US third parties, as does the *Electoral College*, and the demanding ballot-access rules that operate in many states.

■ *TIP* Though third parties rarely win US elections, they can affect the outcome (e.g. *Ralph Nader* in 2000) or influence the policies of more mainstream candidates (e.g. *Perot* in 1992).

■ *COMPARATIVE* In the UK, the term 'minor parties' is generally preferred to 'third parties'. Issue-based parties such as UKIP and the Green Party have done well in recent years as have regional parties such as the SNP — particularly in respect of elections to devolved institutions.

Thirteenth Amendment (1865): prohibited *slavery*.

● It also banned other forms of involuntary servitude, unless imposed as a punishment for crimes for which the individual in question had been duly convicted.

● The amendment was ratified following the defeat of the Confederate states in the American *Civil War*.

Thomas, Clarence (1948–): an associate justice of the US *Supreme Court*, nominated by *George H. W. Bush* in 1991 and confirmed by the US *Senate* (52:48).

● Thomas was the second *African-American* to serve on the Court. The first was Thurgood Marshall, the man Thomas replaced.

● Thomas's confirmation hearings provoked controversy as a result of the allegations of sexual harassment levelled at him by former colleague Anita Hill.

● Such allegations and the fear that Thomas might be willing to overturn the 1973 *Roe* v *Wade* ruling, led groups such as the *National Organization of Women (NOW)* to campaign, albeit unsuccessfully, against his confirmation.

t

- Thomas became part of a solid conservative block on the Court alongside *Antonin Scalia* and the then chief justice *William H. Rehnquist*.

Thurmond, Strom (1902–2003): a former governor of South Carolina and long-serving member of the US *Senate* representing the same state. Thurmond also stood as a pro-segregationist candidate in the 1948 presidential election, under a 'States Rights Party' banner.

- He won four southern states in the 1948 presidential election. In addition, Tennessee *Electoral College* member Preston Parks cast his ballot for Thurmond, rather than the candidate he was supposed to support, Democrat incumbent *Harry Truman* (see *rogue elector*). In total, Thurmond secured 39 Electoral College votes.
- Thurmond was originally elected to the Senate as a Democrat (1954–64) but was later re-elected as a Republican (1964–2003). At the time of his retirement he was the longest ever serving member of the Senate.
- He conducted the longest ever *filibuster* by a US Senator, in opposition to the *Civil Rights Act* of 1957. He spoke for 24 hours and 18 minutes.

■ *TIP* Though Thurmond remained politically conservative, his views on race softened with age. By the time of his last election to the US Senate in 1996, he was able to secure around 22% of the black vote in South Carolina. Shortly after he died in 2003 it was also revealed that Thurmond had fathered a daughter by an *African-American* maid in 1925.

ticket: a collective term referring to a party's presidential and vice-presidential candidates.

- Since the *Twelfth Amendment* (1804) the two posts have been elected jointly. Prior to that the candidate coming second in the *Electoral College* took on the role of *vice-president*.
- Some use the term 'ticket' more broadly to refer to all of the candidates a party might have running for office on election day. See also *split-ticket voting*.

■ *e.g.* In 2004 the Democrats ran with a Kerry–Edwards ticket whereas the Republicans stuck with the Bush–Cheney ticket that had secured victory 4 years earlier.

■ *TIP* See also *balanced ticket*.

Tonkin Gulf Resolution: see *Gulf of Tonkin Resolution*.

Tower, John (1925–91): a former US Senator who later chaired the Tower Commission inquiry into the *Iran-Contra* affair. Tower was nominated as defense secretary by *George H. W. Bush* in 1989 but was rejected by the *Senate* following allegations of heavy drinking, womanising and a possible conflict of interests relating to his outside business interests.

tracking poll: in-house poll taken by a candidate's team at regular intervals during a campaign as a means of evaluating his/her electoral strategy and refocusing the candidate's message where new issues have come to the fore.

Treasury Department: one of the three original *executive departments* that were established in 1789, the Treasury was created to deal with government revenues. It is headed by a secretary to the Treasury who holds *cabinet* rank.

treaty: a formal agreement between one or more nations. In the USA, treaties are negotiated by the president and ratified by a two-thirds majority vote in the US *Senate*.

● The difficulty in achieving the two-thirds Senate majority required for *ratification* of treaties has resulted in a rise in the number of so-called *executive agreements*.

■ *TIP* President *Carter* argued that it would make more sense to require a two-thirds Senate majority vote to reject a treaty negotiated by the president, than it does to require the same majority to ratify one.

■ *COMPARATIVE* In the UK, the prerogative powers allow the prime minister to conclude treaties without the need for formal ratification.

trimester: refers to a period of 3 months in the course of a pregnancy.

● A normal pregnancy is divided into three trimesters.

● The US *Supreme Court* has ruled that restrictions on women accessing *abortions* in the first trimester are more likely to be ruled *unconstitutional* than those that seek to limit the availability of the procedure in the third trimester (i.e. when the foetus is viable).

● This is part of a process by which the rights of the prospective mother and the rights of the foetus are balanced over the course of the pregnancy.

Truman, Harry S. (1884–1972): the *vice-president* to *Franklin D. Roosevelt* who became the thirty-third US *president* upon Roosevelt's death in 1945. Re-elected in his own right in 1948, Truman served until 1953, having decided not to run in the 1952 presidential election following a bad showing in the *New Hampshire primary*.

● Truman's foreign policy was shaped by the start of the Cold War. The so-called 'Truman doctrine' set out a policy of containment where the US looked to actively stop the spread of communism through both economic and military means.

■ *e.g.* The Marshall Plan provided the financial support needed to re-build a Western Europe laid waste by the Second World War. Truman's reaction to the Berlin Blockade and the North Korean invasion of South Korea signalled a willingness on the part of the US to face down the threat of communism.

■ *TIP* He is often remembered for his use of the phrase 'the buck stops here'.

Tsongas, Paul (1941–97): a *Democratic Party* member of the US *Senate*, representing Massachusetts, Tsongas later sought his party's nomination in the 1992 presidential election.

● Tsongas retired from the Senate in 1984, having been diagnosed with cancer, but returned to run for the Democratic Party nomination in the 1992 presidential election.

- Although Tsongas beat *Bill Clinton* in the *New Hampshire primary*, his challenge fell away thereafter. Citing a lack of campaign contributions as one reason for his failure, Tsongas later remarked, 'if money is the mother's milk of politics, ours didn't turn up until March'.
- Tsongas died of cancer in 1997.
- **■ TIP** Clinton's success in securing the Democratic Party nomination following his early defeat by Tsongas in the New Hampshire primary led to him being dubbed 'the comeback kid'.

turnout: in the USA, the *Federal Election Commission* has traditionally measured turnout as a percentage of Voting Age Population (VAP), as opposed to a percentage of registered voters.

- As a significant minority of those who are of voting age are either not eligible to vote or not registered to vote, turnout figures based on VAP tend to be artificially low.
- **■ e.g.** Turnout as a percentage of VAP was only 51.3% in the 2000 presidential election. This is partly a result of the fact that only 76% of eligible voters were registered to vote in 2000.
- **■ COMPARATIVE** In the UK, where voter registration is compulsory, turnout is measured as a percentage of registered voters. If one calculates turnout in the 2000 presidential election using the same measure, it would have been around 68% — which compares favourably with the 59% turnout recorded in the 2001 UK general election.

Twelfth Amendment (1804): altered the process for electing the *president* and *vice-president*, e.g. introduced the practice of electing the vice-president on a joint ticket alongside the president as opposed taking on the role of 'deputy' simply by being the person who came second in the *Electoral College* vote.

Twentieth Amendment (1933): formally *entrenched* a number of key dates relating to precisely when the terms of members of *Congress* and the *president* commenced and ended. It also put in place rules to deal with a number of scenarios where the death of an elected individual might otherwise leave a seat vacant.

Twenty-Fifth Amendment (1967): sets out the circumstances in which the *vice-president* shall become *president* and puts in place a mechanism by which a new vice-president should be chosen in such an eventuality.

- This amendment also allows the vice-president to take over temporarily where the president declares himself 'unable to discharge the powers or duties of his office' or where the vice-president and a majority of the *cabinet* arrive at a similar judgement

Twenty-First Amendment (1933): repealed the *Eighteenth Amendment* (1919), thereby ending the Prohibition of alcohol.

Twenty-Fourth Amendment (1964): prohibited the use of a *poll tax.*

Twenty-Second Amendment (1951): imposed a two-term limit on US presidents.

- This amendment was seen by many as a somewhat belated response to the fact that *Franklin D. Roosevelt* had been elected for four consecutive terms in the 1930s and 1940s.
- *e.g.* In recent years both *Ronald Reagan* (served 1981–89) and *Bill Clinton* (served 1993–2001) might realistically have been expected to seek third terms had the Twenty-Second Amendment not prevented them from doing so.
- *TIP* Though this amendment appears to limit an individual to a maximum of 8 years in the White House, it is actually possible to serve nearly 10 years if a *vice-president* takes over just beyond the mid-way point in the *president*'s term, and is subsequently elected for two full terms.
- *COMPARATIVE* No such term limits exist in respect of the UK prime minister. Margaret Thatcher famously said that she intended to 'go on and on', and Tony Blair served for a decade at Number 10.

Twenty-Seventh Amendment (1992): requires an election to have taken place before any previously agreed change in the pay of House Members or Senators can take effect.

Twenty-Sixth Amendment (1971): lowered the voting age to 18 nationwide.

- The *Voting Rights Act (1970)* had earlier granted those aged 18 and over the right to vote in federal elections.

Twenty-Third Amendment (1961): afforded Washington DC a number of *Electoral College* votes equal to that which the *district* would have if it were a US state — with the proviso that it should never have a greater number of Electoral College votes than the least populous state.

- Washington DC has held three Electoral College votes since the *ratification* of this amendment.

Tyler, John (1790–1862): the tenth US *president*, 1841–45.

unanimous consent agreement: in general terms, refers to any motion that the *House of Representatives* or the *Senate* adopt without any member objecting.

- Such agreements are useful because they provide a way of dealing with uncontroversial matters quickly and efficiently, thus freeing up valuable time in the *legislature*.
- The term is used more specifically to refer to the agreements between the *majority and minority leaders* in the Senate regarding the timetabling of bills within the chamber and the way in which they will be treated on the floor.
- ▓ *TIP* In the House of Representatives the role of timetabling is performed by the *Rules Committee*.

unconstitutional: any action or statute, whether by state or federal government, that is deemed to violate the provisions of the US *Constitution*.

- Such actions are normally found to be unconstitutional as a result of action in the US *Supreme Court* or other senior courts.
- ▓ *e.g.* In the case of *Brown v Board of Education (1954)* the US Supreme Court found the practice of segregation in schools unconstitutional because it violated the *Fourteenth Amendment's* guarantee of equal protection under the law.

Union: the northern states of the USA during the *Civil War.*

union: an organisation of workers within a particular trade or profession formed with the aim of advancing its members' collective interests.

- Unions often form national peak organisations as a means of advancing the cause of all unionised workers within a country.
- ▓ *e.g.* the *American Federation of Labour and Congress of Industrial Organisations (AFL-CIO)* is the largest federation of unions in the USA.
- ▓ *COMPARATIVE* In the UK, the Trades Union Congress (TUC) is the dominant peak organisation representing unionised workers.

unitary executive: advanced by *John Yoo* and others, a justification of the power of the *executive* based on the belief that the original intent of those who framed the *Constitution* had been to create a powerful chief executive exercising sole executive power.

- By using the executive's *enumerated* and *implied powers* to their full extent, successive White House incumbents had been able to enhance their control over government.
- The use of *executive orders* and other directives has been crucial, as has the president's willingness to use *executive privilege* to classify executive records.
- *Congress* and the *Supreme Court* have allowed the *president* further extra-constitutional (even *unconstitutional*) powers since the 1970s.

▦ *e.g.* In domestic policy, the Republican Congress granted the president a form of *line item veto* over legislation. In foreign affairs, the *War Powers Act (1973)* and the Authorization of Military Force (AUMF) of 18 September 2001 meant that though Congress may retain the power to declare war, the president is free to wage war without a formal declaration.

▦ *TIP* Proponents of unitary executive theory argue that Congress's power to check the president's power within the executive branch is strictly limited. This argument has been used to question the constitutionality of *independent regulatory commissions* created by the *legislature,* and also to support the right of the executive to order the use of torture against terrorist suspects.

United States v Drayton (2002): a case in which the US *Supreme Court* ruled that the *Fourth Amendment's* prohibition of 'unreasonable searches and seizures' did not demand that passengers on a Greyhound bus be told of their right not to cooperate with the police officers who wanted to search them.

▦ *TIP* The case was significant in that it gave police greater freedom to search those travelling on all forms of public transport in the wake of *9/11.*

United States v Eichman (1990): a case in which the US *Supreme Court* struck down a US statute banning *flag desecration* on the grounds that it violated the *First Amendment's* protection of free speech.

- *Congress* had passed the Act in response to the Court's landmark ruling in *Texas v Johnson (1989).*

United States v Lopez (1995): a case in which the US *Supreme Court* declared the Gun-Free School Zones Act (1990) *unconstitutional.*

- The Act had made it an offence for individuals to possess a firearm in an area they knew or could be reasonably be expected to know was a school zone.
- The Court argued that *Congress* had exceeded the power given to it in Article 1, section 8 of the *Constitution* when attempting to limit the *Second Amendment's* right to 'bear arms'.

United States v Richard Nixon (1974): a case in which the US *Supreme Court* ordered the then President *Richard Nixon* to hand over the recordings known as the *White House Tapes* to the official investigation into the *Watergate scandal.*

- Nixon had argued that he could withhold the tapes under his *executive privilege.*
- The Court's decision precipitated Nixon's resignation 4 days later.

Utah: the forty-fifth state; joined the *Union* in 1896.

Van Buren, Martin (1782–1862): the eighth US president, 1837–41.

Ventura, Jesse (1951–): a former pro-wrestler, actor and one-term *third-party* governor of Minnesota (1999–2003).

● Ventura defeated credible Republican and Democratic Party candidates in the 1998 gubernatorial election (Norm Coleman and Hubert H. Humphrey III respectively).

Vermont: the fourteenth state; joined the *Union* in 1791.

Versailles Treaty: see *Woodrow Wilson*.

veto: literally meaning 'I forbid' (from the Latin), the power of the *president* to block measures passed by both the *House of Representatives* and the *Senate*.

● Under the *Constitution* the president must either sign a bill or return it to *Congress* unsigned within 10 congressional working days, along with a written note of his objections. Failure to do so results in the measure becoming law automatically.

● This 'veto' can be overridden with a two-thirds 'supermajority' in each chamber of Congress.

● The president can also 'pocket' and thereby kill bills that are passed to him within 10 working days of the end of a congressional session. Congress will look to avoid this 'pocket veto' by ensuring that the bills the president may want to pocket are sent to him in good time.

▇ *e.g.* Bill Clinton used the regular veto on 36 occasions and was overridden twice. He only used the pocket veto once during his 8 years in office.

▇ *TIP* The president must deal with the entire bill presented to him. He does not have a *line-item veto*. See also *signing statement*.

vice-president: part of the *ticket* in the quadrennial presidential election, the vice-president is the only member of the *executive* other than the *president* who is elected.

● Candidates for the position of vice-president have to meet the same constitutional requirements of age, citizenship and residency that apply to the president.

● The vice-president is the first in line to replace the president in the event of his/her resignation (e.g. *Nixon*) or death (e.g. *Kennedy*).

- Under the *Twenty-Fifth Amendment* the vice-president may also take over where the president declares himself unable to discharge his duties or where the vice-president and the majority of the *cabinet* believe that he/she is unable to do so.
- The vice-president has the title of president of the *Senate* and can cast a deciding vote where the Senate is tied, e.g. *Dick Cheney* did so when pushing through *George W. Bush*'s $1.6 trillion tax cut in April 2001.
- The post of vice-president is often seen as a training ground for presidents.
- ■ *e.g.* Richard Nixon had served as vice-president under *Dwight Eisenhower*.
- ■ *TIP* The Office of Vice President has undergone a renaissance in recent years. *Clinton* gave *Al Gore* a significant role in areas such as the *NAFTA* negotiations. Under George W. Bush, Dick Cheney was cast as virtual 'prime minister' to George W. Bush's 'head of state'.

Vietnam War (1959–75): resulted from the efforts of the Ho Chi Minh-led Communist Democratic Republic of Vietnam (which controlled North Vietnam) and its supporters in the South (the Viet Cong) to overthrow the western-backed South Vietnamese government, the Republic of Vietnam.

- Most often remembered for the period between 1965 and 1973, which saw a full deployment of US ground forces and the carpet-bombing of North Vietnam by the United State Air Force. See *Gulf of Tonkin Resolution*.
- Most US troops withdrew in 1973 as a result of the Paris Peace Accords.
- The war finally ended in 1975 when the North captured the southern capital of Saigon.
- ■ *TIP* The US fear of communism in southeast Asia was based on their belief in the domino theory, the idea that communism would spread from state to state until it reached USA's borders.

Virginia: the tenth state; joined the *Union* in 1788.

- Virginia was the largest state at the time of the *Philadelphia Convention* in 1787 and it sent the largest number of delegates (later known as the *Founding Fathers*) to negotiate the new constitutional settlement.
- A number of Virginian Founding Fathers went on to serve as US president in the early years of the *Union*.
- ■ *e.g.* *George Washington*, *Thomas Jefferson*, and *James Madison*.

Virginia Plan: advanced by a number of larger states at the *Philadelphia Convention* of 1787, the idea that seats in the new *legislature* might be allocated between states in broad proportion to population.

- The smaller states favoured the *New Jersey Plan*.
- ■ *TIP* Both the larger and the smaller states were eventually able to agree as a result of the *Connecticut Compromise*.

voter registration: a process by which those eligible to vote are formally entered onto the electoral register that will be used during a given electoral cycle.

- In recent years there have been a number of attempts to increase levels of voter registration in the USA. See *motor voter law*.

- Under the *Tenth Amendment* to the US *Constitution* states have traditionally been given a good deal of freedom to set their own rules regarding voter registration.
- **e.g.** In the 2000 presidential election, for example, voters in Missouri had to register to vote at least 28 days ahead of the election, whereas in Idaho it was possible for voters to register on election day itself if they could provide the necessary documentation.
- **TIP** Levels of voter registration differ significantly according to factors such as race, e.g. in 2000 only 34.9% of Hispanics were registered compared to 70% amongst non-Hispanic white voters.
- **COMPARATIVE** UK households are legally required to complete voter registration forms. Failure to do so can result in a fine.

voter registration drive: any effort — whether organised by a political party, a *pressure group*, or any other organisation — to increase the proportion of eligible citizens who register to vote.

- Such drives often target specific groups within society, e.g. ethnic groups, age groups or religious groups.
- **e.g.** The *Moral Majority* claimed to have registered 10 million new voters 'for' Republican *Ronald Reagan* between 1980 and 1984. Rock the Vote tried to increase levels of registration and *turnout* amongst young voters.
- **TIP** Voter registration drives fell within a category of activities that could once be funded using *soft money* that was unregulated by the *Federal Election Campaign Act (1974)*.

voting behaviour: refers to established patterns in the way in which individuals or groups of individuals vote in elections.

- There are a number of clear long-term patterns in US voting behaviour. Black voters, for example, have tended to vote Democrat in the modern era, as have women and those on low incomes.
- **e.g.** In the 2004 presidential election the Democratic presidential candidate *John Kerry* secured the support of 88% of black voters, 51% of women, and 63% of those with a family income of less that $15,000 per annum.
- **TIP** Many of the voting models that have been applied to the study of UK voting behaviour can also be applied to the USA.

Voting Rights Act (1965): a federal statute that outlawed the use of literacy tests as a requirement for voter registration and empowered federal government officials to register voters in states with low levels of ethnic minority voter registration.

- Literacy tests had been used as a means of disenfranchising black voters in some southern states.
- The Act came in the wake of the *Twenty-Fourth Amendment* to the US *Constitution* (1964), which had outlawed a number of other devices designed to restrict the ethnic minority vote. Taken together these reforms had a dramatic effect on voter registration in many southern states.

e.g. In Alabama, the proportion of eligible black citizens registered to vote rose from 19.3% before the 1964 Act to 51% in 1968. In Mississippi the rise was even more marked (6.7% up to 59.8%).

Voting Rights Act (1970): a federal statute that extended the right to vote in federal elections to those aged 18 and over.

- The *Twenty-Sixth Amendment* to the US *Constitution* extended this voting age to all elections in 1971.
- These measures increased the size of the US *electorate* by around 11 million voters.

 COMPARATIVE In the UK, the voting age was reduced to 18 by the 1969 Representation of the People Act.

Waco: see *Branch Davidians.*

Wallace, George (1919–98): former governor of Alabama and failed candidate for the Democratic presidential nomination in 1964, 1972 and 1976. Wallace is best remembered for his *third-party* candidacy in the presidential election of 1968.

- Despite his later recantation, Wallace is often remembered as a segregationist.
- He hoped to win enough *Electoral College* votes to result in a 'hung college'. He believed that such an outcome would give the southern states sufficient leverage to halt the federal government's programme of desegregation.
- Wallace's campaign undermined the Republican candidate *Richard Nixon*'s '*Southern Strategy*' and brought the Democrat *Hubert Humphrey* within a few hundred thousand votes of securing victory.
- Though his candidacy did not result in the hung Electoral College he had hoped for, Wallace did win five states (Alabama, Arkansas, Georgia, Louisiana, and Mississippi).
- One of North Carolina's Electoral College members, Dr Lloyd Bailey, also cast his ballot in favour of Wallace rather than the candidate he was supposed to support, the Republican Richard Nixon.

TIP Wallace's success in securing 46 Electoral College votes, in spite of the fact that he only secured 13.5% of the popular vote nationally, resulted from the fact that his votes were concentrated in the South.

Wallace v Jaffree (1985): a case in which the US *Supreme Court* struck down an Alabama law that allowed a moment's silence for voluntary prayer on the grounds that it violated the Establishment Clause of the *First Amendment* to the US *Constitution*.

Wall Street Crash: the cataclysmic collapse of the US stock-market on Wall Street. Often referred to as 'Black Tuesday', the Crash took place on 29 October 1929.

- The Crash is widely regarded as marking the start of the *Great Depression*.

War Powers Act (1973): sometimes referred to as the War Powers Resolution, a federal statute passed to limit the prevalence of *presidential wars*. The Act is widely ignored by presidents and *Congress* alike, and is of questionable constitutionality.

- In 1971 Senator Barry Goldwater remarked that 'we [the US] have only been in 5 declared wars out of over 150 that we have fought'. A good example of an undeclared war is the *Vietnam War* (see *Gulf of Tonkin Resolution*).
- The Act requires the president 'in every possible instance' to inform Congress at the start of hostilities and to consult regularly with the *legislature* until the forces had been withdrawn.
- The president is only allowed to use the armed forces for 60 days without congressional approval and then has a further 30 days to withdraw forces if that approval is not ultimately forthcoming.
- This raised the possibility that presidents could wage short-term wars without ever securing congressional support for a formal declaration of war.

■ *TIP* Though the War Powers Act set out to limit the president's power to wage war without formal declaration by Congress, it could be seen to have actually granted the president extra-constitutional, or even *unconstitutional* powers. It has survived largely as a result of the fact that it has never been properly tested before the US *Supreme Court*. See also the *Case Act (1972)* and the *Budget and Impoundment Control Act (1974)*.

■ *COMPARATIVE* In the UK, the prime minister is free to lead the UK into war without parliamentary approval under the prerogative powers.

War on Terror: launched by *George W. Bush* in the wake of the attacks on *9/11*, a general statement of intent regarding those who the USA saw as terrorists, and the nations who offered them shelter and material support.

- Bush also spoke of an 'axis of evil', consisting of those nations said to be sponsoring global terrorism.
- Some commentators felt that the use of the word 'war' was significant as it made it easier for the president to justify certain actions that might otherwise appear unreasonable.
- Critics also argued that the term was something of a misnomer as it was impossible to declare war on an abstract concept.

Warren, Earl (1891–1974): former chief justice of the US *Supreme Court* (1954–69), previously governor of California.

- Warren was appointed associate justice by President *Dwight Eisenhower* in October 1953. This was a recess appointment, one that was never confirmed by the US *Senate* due to the fact that they were not sitting at the time of the appointment.
- Eisenhower then nominated Warren as chief justice in January 1954, following the death of the incumbent Fred M. Vinson. Warren's appointment as chief justice was confirmed by the Senate in March 1954.
- Warren's appointment was seen largely as reward for the work that the then governor of California had done for Eisenhower in winning the *Republican Party*'s nomination in the 1952 presidential election.

- To Eisenhower's surprise Warren became one of the most liberal and activist chief justices in the Court's history.
- **e.g.** the *Brown* v *Board of Education* case of 1954. See also *judicial activism* and *loose constructionism*.
- **TIP** The fact that Warren turned out to be a far different kind of chief justice than Eisenhower anticipated is a good example of judicial independence and of the *security of tenure* enjoyed by those on the Supreme Court. Eisenhower later described Warren's appointment as 'the biggest damn-fool mistake I ever made'.

Washington: the forty-second state; joined the *Union* in 1889.

TIP It is important not to confuse Washington State with Washington DC.

Washington DC: see *District of Columbia*.

Washington, George (1732–99): the first US president, 1789–97.

- Washington had been a leading American general in the *War of Independence*.
- He was later one of the *Founding Fathers*, attending the *Philadelphia Convention* (1787) as part of the Virginia delegation. Washington was named as the president of the Convention and presented the new *Constitution* to the various states for their *ratification*.
- He was chosen as the first *president* of the United States in April 1789.

WASP: an acronym for White Anglo-Saxon Protestant.

***Watchtower Bible and Tract Society of New York Inc.* v *Village of Stratton, Ohio* (2002):** a case in which the US *Supreme Court* struck down a local law passed in Stratton, Ohio. The regulation required people seeking to go from door to door to first obtain a permit. The Court argued that such a requirement violated the *First Amendment*.

Watergate scandal: resulting from the investigation into a break-in at the head-quarters of the *Democratic National Committee* in the Watergate Hotel, Washington DC, that took place during the 1972 presidential election campaign.

- Those involved in the break-in included former members of the CIA and had been funded by the *Committee to Re-elect the President (CREEP)*, the fundraising arm of incumbent Republican President *Richard Nixon*'s 1972 election campaign.
- *Washington Post* reporters *Bob Woodward* and *Carl Bernstein* uncovered a link between the Nixon campaign and the burglary, but also stumbled upon evidence of more widespread corruption within the Nixon administration.
- Nixon was re-elected in 1972 but was effectively forced to resign in 1974 following the US *Supreme Court*'s decision to order the release of the White House Tapes (see *United States* v *Richard Nixon, 1974*). Had he failed to resign it is likely that he would have been impeached, convicted and removed from office.

TIP The suffix 'gate' has since been attached to a number of subsequent scandals, e.g. *Monicagate*.

Ways and Means Committee: a *House of Representatives* committee that has broad jurisdiction over all revenue-raising measures.

- All bills concerned with taxation must go through the Ways and Means Committee.
- The committee also plays a role in overseeing a number of key government programmes, e.g. *MEDICARE.*

Webster v Reproductive Health Services (1989): a case in which the US *Supreme Court* recognised that 'life begins at conception' and that the 'gestational age, weight and lung maturity' of the foetus (i.e. whether it could survive independently of the mother) could be tested in the case of a woman believed to be 20 or more weeks pregnant. This case was widely seen as a narrowing of the constitutional right to *abortion* established in *Roe* v *Wade (1973).*

West Virginia: the thirty-fifth state; joined the *Union* in 1963.

West Wing: the nerve-centre of the US presidency, set over two floors in an extension to the White House demanded by *Theodore Roosevelt.*

- It houses the Oval Office, the Cabinet Room, the Roosevelt Room, the Situation Room, and the Press Briefing Room.
- Around 40–50 of the president's senior staff also have offices in the West Wing.
- **TIP** Most of the president's staff are now housed in the Eisenhower Executive Office Building, which is adjacent to the West Wing.
- **COMPARATIVE** Some argue that changes in the size, organisation and location of many of the bodies that comprise the Cabinet Office and Prime Minister's Office have resulted in the creation of a 'UK West Wing' in all but name.

whip: party official with a broad responsibility for maintaining party unity within *Congress.*

- Individuals holding the titles of minority whip and majority whip exist in both the *House of Representatives* and the *Senate.*
- **e.g.** In 2007 the majority whip in the House of Representatives was James Clyburn (Democrat, South Carolina) and the minority whip was Roy Blunt (Republican, Missouri). In the Senate the majority whip was Richard Durbin (Democrat, Illinois) and the minority whip was Trent Lott (Republican, Mississippi).
- **COMPARATIVE** In the UK, the term applies to a document detailing a party's positions on parliamentary business in the week ahead, as well as to an individual who tries to enforce these positions.

White House Staff (WHS): a collective term referring to the president's closest and most senior *aides.*

- The WHS is headed by and answerable to the president's *chief of staff.*
- It provides the interface between the president and the wider *federal bureaucracy* beyond the White House.
- The Congressional Liaison Staff, part of the WHS, manages relations between the White House and the *legislature.*

White House Tapes: see *United States* v *Richard Nixon (1974).*

***William Jefferson Clinton* v *Paula Corbin Jones* (1997):** a case in which the US *Supreme Court* ruled that President *Bill Clinton* had to give evidence in a case relating to his alleged sexual harassment of Paula Corbin Jones during his time as governor of Arkansas.

Wilson, Woodrow (1856–1924): the twenty-eighth US *president* (Democrat), 1913–1921.

- Remembered for his contribution to the peace negotiations that resulted in the Versailles Treaty (1919).
- Wilson's 14-points proposed a range of measures including the principle of settling national borders on the basis of 'self-determination'.
- A keen advocate for the creation of a League of Nations, Wilson was frustrated by the *Senate*'s rejection of the Treaty of Versailles, which had the effect of preventing the USA from joining the embryonic organisation.

Wisconsin: the thirtieth state; joined the *Union* in 1848.

Woodward, Bob (1943–): a reporter with the *Washington Post* who, along with *Carl Bernstein*, exposed the full scale of the *Watergate scandal* between 1972 and 1974.

Wright, Jim (1922–): a former *Speaker of the House of Representatives* who was forced to resign tearfully in 1989 when the House Ethics Committee announced that it would be charging him with 69 violations of the House's ethics rules.

- The scandal centred on royalties Wright had received in respect of his book, *Reflections of a Public Man*.
- Some saw the allegations against Wright as 'pay-back' from enemies he had made during his time as House Speaker.
- *e.g.* Wright had annoyed many leading Republicans over his vocal opposition to aid for the Contras. See *Iran-Contra affair*.

write-in candidate: where voters can support an individual whose name does not appear on the ballot by writing the name of their chosen candidate into the space provided on the ballot paper.

- The existence of the write-in option in elections in some US states is a carry-over from a time when it was the norm for ballot papers to be blank.
- Nowadays write-in candidates are most often those who were not registered in time to have their names printed on the official ballot paper.

Wyoming: the forty-fourth state; joined the *Union* in 1890.

Youngstown Sheet and Tube Company v Sawyer (1952): a case in which the US *Supreme Court* ruled that President *Truman*'s commerce secretary Charles Sawyer had acted unconstitutionally when deploying federal troops as a means of breaking a nationwide strike in the steel industry.

Yoo, John (1967–): known for his 2005 book, *The Powers of War and Peace: The Constitution and Foreign Affairs After 9/11*, Yoo is one of a number of writers who have developed the concept of the *unitary executive*.

YUMPIE: an expansion of an acronym referring to young, upwardly mobile professionals. See *YUPPIE*.

YUPPIE: an expansion of an acronym referring to young urban professionals. The term is commonly associated with young, high-income professionals who enjoy an ostentatious lifestyle.

Zelman v *Simmons-Harris* (2002): a case in which the US *Supreme Court* upheld an Ohioan programme that helped parents to send their children to religious and private schools by providing transferable 'school vouchers'.
- The judgement appeared to undermine the constitutional separation of church and state enshrined in the Establishment Clause of the *First Amendment*.